Praise for

HUCK

A *USA Today* Fall Book Pick
A *Good Morning America* Great Fall Read Pick

"Elder is a gifted writer whose story is sure to tug on heart-strings and leave readers with a renewed belief in the kindness of strangers."   —*Publishers Weekly*

"It's about hope, it's about fear, it's about triumph. . . . I guarantee you, you'll feel better about everything after you read this."   —David Letterman

"This story takes place in the most familiar places—a doctor's office, a family's kitchen, a suburban high school, and the woods out back. It's a modern-day myth that happened to be true. It's a story in which wonderful things occurred because people believed in themselves and in each other. It's a story about the power of love to change our world."

—Caroline Kennedy

"A story of how healing the love of a pet can be and of faith that good things can still happen when people pull together— a true, feel-good read."　　　　—Patricia Cornwell, author of the

Scarpetta series and dog lover

"*Huck* is the *Dewey* of the canine world. The dog is a delight— even my cat, Norton, would have been charmed (after a hiss or two)—and the book itself is lovely and inspiring. I rate it 5 barks."　　　—Peter Gethers, author of *The Cat Who Went to Paris* and *The Cat Who'll Live Forever*

"Janet Elder's wonderful story of Huck reminds us that the best stories about dogs are really about people or, in this case, community. Few things in America these days can bring people together more than a shared love of dogs. Dogs enter our lives for all kinds of reasons, and Huck entered Janet

Elder's life for one of the most important. This is a wonderful story, gripping and heartwarming. And I can't say I've ever read a dog story with a more meaningful or uplifting ending. You are likely to cry some happy tears."

—Jon Katz, author of *Soul of a Dog: Reflections on the Spirits of the Animals of Bedlam Farm*

"This dog story made me feel good about people, families, and New Jersey." —Roy Blount Jr.

"Puppies have always been better than people. Now comes a book where a puppy makes people better people. Pet it, feed it, even read it. You'll love it—and become a better person."

—Dan Jenkins, sportswriter/novelist

"Janet Elder and her family fell in love with their dog, Huck.... You'll fall in love with them. A wonderful, inspiring book." —Deirdre Imus

HUCK

HUCK

*The Remarkable True Story of How One Lost Puppy
Taught a Family—and a Whole Town—About Hope
and Happy Endings*

JANET ELDER

BROADWAY PAPERBACKS
NEW YORK

BROADWAY

All rights reserved.
Published in the United States by Broadway Paperbacks,
an imprint of the Crown Publishing Group, a division of
Random House, Inc., New York.
www.crownpublishing.com

BROADWAY PAPERBACKS and its logo, a letter B bisected on the
diagonal, are trademarks of Random House, Inc.

Originally published in hardcover in slightly different form
in the United States by Broadway Books, an imprint of the
Crown Publishing Group, a division of Random House, Inc.,
New York, in 2010.

Library of Congress Cataloging-in-Publication Data
Elder, Janet.
The remarkable true story of how one lost puppy taught a
family—and a whole town—about hope and happy endings /
by Janet Elder.
1. Miniature poodle—New Jersey—Ramsey—Anecdotes.
2. Puppies—New Jersey—Ramsey—Anecdotes.   3. Human-
animal relationships—Anecdotes.   I. Title.
SF429.M57E43 2010
636.72'80922—dc22   2010002021

ISBN 978-0-7679-3135-9
eISBN 978-0-307-71616-3

PRINTED IN THE UNITED STATES OF AMERICA

Map by Martie Holmer
Cover design by Laura Duffy
Cover photography by Lawrence Pinsky

10 9 8 7 6 5 4

First Paperback Edition

For Michael and Rich

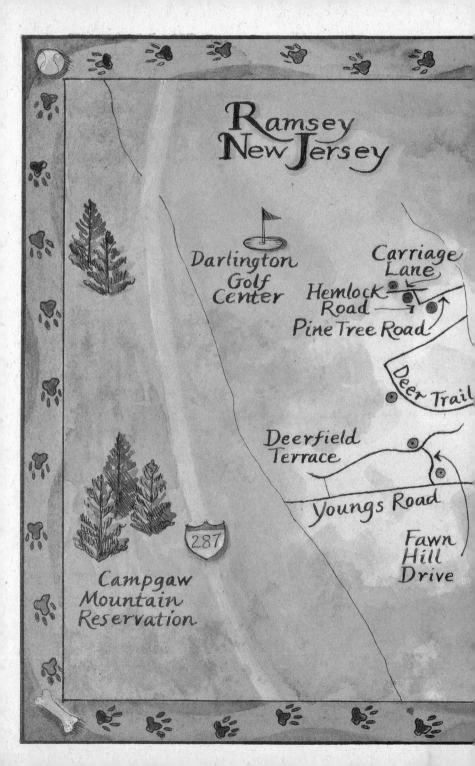

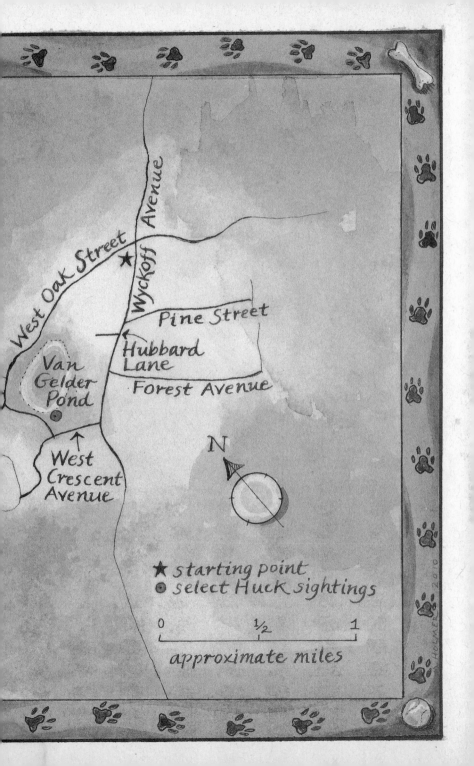

West Oak Street

Wyckoff Avenue

Pine Street

Hubbard Lane

Van Gelder Pond

Forest Avenue

West Crescent Avenue

N

★ starting point
⦿ select Huck sightings

0   ½   1

approximate miles

$1,000 CASH
REWARD

LOST DOG!
3/23/06
RAMSEY/MAHWAH VIC.

917-555-5555
201-555-5555

OR LOCAL POLICE
REDDISH BROWN TOY POODLE PUPPY WITH
SHAGGY "PUPPYCUT"

PLEASE: HEARTBROKEN BOY

"HUCK"
IF SEEN, CALMLY SAY: "CREAM CHEESE, HUCK." BRING HIM
INTO YOUR HOME *PLEASE. AND CALL US, PLEASE!*

HUCK

Chapter 1

I DEVELOPED A LOT OF TALISMANS when I had cancer—a pair of pink-and-white antique-looking earrings a close friend brought from Paris; a delicate gold bracelet with a single charm inscribed LIFE from a woman I hardly knew who said she admired my bravery; a purple bear holding the word MOM my son, Michael, gave me when he visited me in the hospital; a note from my brother-in-law, scribbled on yellow lined paper, quoting one of the many doctors I had seen, who asserted, "You will be cured." I kept my lucky charms near me, brought them along to doctor's visits, stared at them in the middle of the night, and held tight to them when I felt vulnerable.

But no talisman was as powerful as a dog named Huck.

Michael said it took him only seven years of begging

to get a dog. For as long as my husband, Rich, and I could remember, every year, Michael's letter to Santa began with a young boy's heartfelt yearnings for a dog. "I just want a puppy to love," he would write in block letters. After years of finding everything under the Christmas tree except a dog, the letter to Santa still asked for a dog but an increasingly disappointed Michael would add parenthetically "even though I know I won't get one."

Michael was relentless in his lobbying effort. When he was ten years old, he had learned how to give a Power-Point presentation in school and showed off his skills at home with a special creation for Rich and me entitled "My Dog."

With Michael seated at the desk in his bedroom and Rich and me standing behind him, one photograph after another of smiling children and playful-looking dogs passed across the computer screen interspersed with outlines of his case. One page entitled "An Amazing Animal" had bullet points, like "You can always get a hug from a dog when you are feeling sad" and "The most loving animal ever." Another page said simply, "A Childhood Without a Dog Is a Sad Thing." The presentation had the desired effect of breaking our hearts. Michael sat there smiling, proud of his accomplishment and certain he had made a convincing argument, asking: "Did you like it?"

I was ready to cry, but I was not ready to get him a dog.

Michael's obsession with animals in general and dogs in particular was my own fault. Somehow, from infancy, I had filled his childhood with endless images of pets, real and imagined, and he fell in love with each and every one. His earliest friends were the cuddly stuffed animals who shared his nursery, Geoffrey Giraffe, Sammy Squirrel, Mamma Duck and Baby Duck, and Snuggles, an enormous golden retriever large enough to take a nap on.

Before Michael was born, while Rich and I were waiting for nine months to tick by, we went out to buy a teddy bear. After rummaging through every neighborhood shop without finding the perfect playmate, we headed downtown to New York City's cathedral of toys—FAO Schwarz.

On our way into the store, we shook hands with a tall man dressed like a toy soldier in a red jacket, blue pants, and a high black hat, standing sentry and greeting customers before they passed through the glass doors. Once inside, we nuzzled bears of all shapes and sizes: black bears, polar bears, panda bears, bears that looked a little too real, and others that were dressed like farmers or clowns. We laughed a lot and finally took home the irresistible, soft, sweet-faced, brown "Fuzzy," to be renamed "Shoshy" by Michael some years later.

We had hoped Shoshy would be Michael's closest compadre, the kind of stuffed animal that moves from bed to closet to attic but never to the trash. But Shoshy, the bear, did not turn out to be Michael's favorite. Shoshy took a backseat to Corky, the dog.

Corky, sandy colored with brown eyes, was small enough to fit in the crook of Michael's neck yet big enough to hug. He had come along in the avalanche of presents from friends and colleagues that accompanied Michael's birth.

As soon as Michael's hands were large enough to grab hold of Corky's paw, Michael and Corky became constant companions. Corky slept alongside Michael, first in his crib, then in his toddler bed, and then in his "big boy" bed.

Corky was the perfect pet. He didn't bark, didn't shed, never had to be walked, and was endlessly tolerant of a little boy throwing him in the air and grabbing him by the tail. Whenever Michael's play got a little too rough and Corky broke a limb, it was easily repaired by Grammy, who just happened to be a retired nurse and quite handy with a needle and thread. Corky was indestructible.

When Michael was a toddler, he had a tendency to run high fevers. Corky was content to lie very still and close. Corky had his temperature taken whenever Michael did. He had his own dish for ice cream. When Michael needed a Band-Aid, Corky got one, too. Michael's imagination had transformed Corky into an integral member of the family. "Mommy, don't forget to kiss Corky good night" or "Daddy, Corky needs milk, too" were the admonitions that served as reminders that Corky was only inanimate to us; he was real to Michael.

The potential for heartbreak was great. Rich and I were so afraid of losing Corky that we bought an identical stuffed dog for Michael to take beyond the confines of home—to the park and on sleepovers, long car rides, and visits to relatives. We told him the new dog was Corky's cousin. It worked pretty well when Michael was a two-year-old toddler but was seen as the bald-faced lie it was by the time he was old enough for nursery school.

Corky and the menagerie in Michael's room were just the beginning.

With writers for parents, Michael's young life was filled with books. They were everywhere: plastic books in the bathtub, cloth books in the crib, cardboard books hanging off the stroller, and shelves filled with books lining the walls. We listened to books on tape in the car.

In the mid-1990s, when Michael was a preschooler, it seemed nearly impossible to buy a children's book that was not about animals. I spent hours perusing bookshops all over the city for picture books with little boys in them, thinking Michael would enjoy identifying with a character like him. But adventures starring little blond-headed boys were in short supply.

Christopher Robin, Winnie the Pooh's loyal, bemused

pal, was too insignificant a character compared with the tale's other stars and their well-defined personas, all of them animals. I always ended up taking animal books to the register, mostly about dogs, *Boomer Goes to School, Where's Spot, My Dog Jessie, Officer Buckle and Gloria, Go Dog Go.*

I'd bring my purchases home and I'd sit in Michael's room on the rocker with the red-and-white polka-dot cushions, Michael and Corky on my lap, the sun streaming through the window; we'd read for hours. We read some of the books so often that in short order I was reciting them rather than reading them. The cadence and rhythms of the books were as much a part of the anthology of words I had wittingly or not committed to memory over the years—*The Lord's Prayer*, the closing sentence of *You Can't Go Home Again*, the opening sentence of the Declaration of Independence, and now the entirety of *The Big Red Barn.*

ı ı ı

Michael was a much longed-for child. I was thirty-six years old, nearly thirty-seven years old by the time Michael was born. Rich was forty-five. I continued to work full-time after Michael was born, leaving him in the care of babysitters. I missed him while I was at work, and I cherished every chance I had to be with him when I was not. During the week, those opportunities came early in the morning and in the evening, the perfect times of the day for a story, and reading together became a treasured ritual.

For Michael's fourth birthday I bought him *McDuff Comes Home,* one of a series of books about an irrepressible white West Highland terrier, or "Westie," named McDuff. In it, McDuff chases a rabbit through hills and streets and gardens, until he finds he has, in fact, run away from home. McDuff's collar snaps off on a branch, making it difficult for even the most well-intentioned stranger to return him to his family and the high life he had been accustomed to, a life of sitting in the garden eating vanilla rice pudding with sliced sausage on top.

It became Michael's favorite book, one that by then he was able to read himself, and one that I trace as the source of his unremitting campaign for a dog. It was after reading this book that he began asking, begging, imploring, and praying for a "McDuff" of his own.

The pleadings to Rich and me would come in spurts. We'd go through a month or so of solid nagging and then Michael would take a few weeks off. Just when I thought he'd put the idea to rest, Michael would come back at us. "I need a dog," or "I just want to have a dog to hug," or "Why can't I have a dog to play catch with or to watch TV with?" or "You had a dog when you were a kid, don't you want a chance to bring back those good old memories?"

It was tough. My answers to Michael's pleas were

always inadequate. From an early age he was able to intellectually outmaneuver Rich and me. Michael was quicker with a rejoinder than we were with new arguments. If he perceived any weakness at all, he'd pounce. I had to be careful not to make one of those promises parents make when they know they are losing an argument and are desperate to change the subject—"maybe when you're older."

I had many moments of weakness and many moments when I nearly caved. But my spine was always stiffened by the seemingly inescapable facts of our family life. Rich works for himself and travels a lot. I was already stretched too thin; my job at *The New York Times* working on the paper's coverage of elections and public opinion was more than a full-time job. Who would walk the dog, especially at night when Rich was away? I couldn't leave Michael asleep and alone at night. We live in a small apartment in New York City; dogs need houses and yards. What about vacations? Who would take care of our dog when we went away? No. No. No. No dog.

The only problem with my thinking was that it failed to recognize that Michael was going to follow his heart no matter what I said. Children have a way of doing that despite their parents. It is just as true when children are four as when they are fourteen. So if Michael could not have a dog, he was going to find a way to have another pet of some sort.

I I I

We were lucky enough to be able to spend part of every summer on Nantucket, an island thirty miles out at sea off the coast of Massachusetts. Rich and I had been doing so since we met. We had eloped on Nantucket. We continued going to Nantucket with Michael and, of course, Corky.

We stayed on the far end of the island in the village of Siasconset (known as 'Sconset to those who know) in a tiny gray-shingled cottage that hadn't had much work done on it since the 1940s. It was filled with old books, mold, young spiders, and character.

The owner of the cottage, Bryce Roberts, was a man well into his seventies who had spent his own childhood summers living there. We appreciated his civility, his old-world manner, his choice of books and art, and his scrupulous attention to the details of how to make the coffeemaker work. He rented the cottage to us below the market price, and that in turn made it possible for us to stay for two or three weeks at a time. We enjoyed the simplicity of life we longed for all the other weeks of the year.

Our uncomplicated Nantucket routines rarely varied day to day or year to year. Every afternoon, we'd pack up bags full of sand toys and changes of clothes for Michael, hats, sunglasses, and sunscreen and head to the beach. We spent hours standing at the ocean's edge, watching Michael first take tentative steps into the ocean and then daring marches toward and speedy retreats from oncoming waves. We dug deep holes for forts, built sand castles, and collected shells.

After the beach, we'd stop at Bartlett's Farm. Everyone who has ever cooked a meal on Nantucket has been to Bartlett's Farm, acres and acres of farmland by the sea, an island fixture since the early 1800s. Somehow the sandy soil and the generations-old care create vegetables that make you wish you never had to buy mass-produced vegetables from a supermarket again. Every Bartlett's ear of corn, every melon, every tomato is a work of art.

The Bartlett family once owned a steer named Babe. They kept him out in one of their fields behind a split-rail fence. Children were desperate to get near Babe, especially Michael. The Bartletts dispensed their unsold ears of corn to anyone who asked to feed Babe. Michael was their most loyal patron. He never tired of feeding Babe and watching the behemoth's drooling, slippery, long, pink tongue suck the entire ear of corn into his mouth, husk and all, smash it with his teeth, and swallow it, seemingly in one bite.

Michael loved Babe. Undoubtedly, Michael was partly responsible for Babe's daunting girth, which kept both Michael and Babe from charging through the fence.

But Babe was not the only attraction at Bartlett's Farm. Michael managed to find his first pet there. As I picked through the tomatoes, Michael would stand by the large wooden table that held hundreds of ears of corn. He'd examine the ears looking for stray inchworms, which he'd then carry on his finger out to the car. The worms usually died before we made it out of the parking lot, so there was never much discussion about the care and feeding of the inchworm. But one summer, when Michael was about five or six, he found a slender, green inchworm that lived longer than a few minutes.

"I'm going to name him 'Inchie,'" Michael said as soon as we pulled the car up the shell-covered driveway behind our cottage. Laughing as Inchie crawled up and down Michael's fingers, Michael insisted we make a home for his newly adopted worm. We rummaged through the kitchen cabinets and found an old mayonnaise jar and then punched some holes in the lid with a screwdriver. There Inchie lived for two days, feeding on grass and leaves. Michael was like a protective parent of a newborn, constantly checking on Inchie. "Do you think he has enough air?" Michael would ask us in earnest, carefully holding the jar and examining the air holes in the lid. "Do you think he knows it is bedtime?" "Is he scared of the dark?"

The older Inchie got, an age measured in hours, the

more attached Michael became. When Inchie died, Michael buried him in the garden in back of our little cottage. He fashioned a rock into a tombstone and wrote "Inchie" on it and stood in front of it with his hand over his heart and said, "Inchie, I will love you forever."

Michael's tenderness toward his newly found and quickly lost pet was so poignant I allowed myself a private daydream of getting Michael a dog. I went so far as to think we might get him a dog while we were on Nantucket. But by the time I walked from the garden through the back door and into the kitchen and picked up the local newspaper, the *Inquirer and Mirror,* off the kitchen table to look for ads for dogs, I had come to my senses and decided against it once again. No dog. We simply could not handle the responsibility.

Being on Nantucket, living life outdoors, gave Michael a chance to be closer to the natural world, freer than he was used to. Every summer, our city child was ecstatic to have a yard, even for just a few weeks. He ran in and out of the house at will, the screen door slamming behind him, something completely alien to a child who lives the rest of the year in a twenty-story apartment building. We all sat outside blowing bubbles, kicking around an oversized beach ball, grilling fish for dinner, and trying to lure one of a family of rabbits out of the shrubbery.

There was a shed just out the back door where the washer and dryer were housed. The deep sink in the shed was where Rich taught Michael the joys of filling a balloon with water and throwing it at each other, something that became a yearly ritual.

Eventually, Michael and a couple of his buddies from the city, Sam Bresnick and his brother Elias, who also spent part of their summers on Nantucket, escalated the ritual into a yearly battle. The arsenal grew larger as the boys did. By the time they were eight, they set out to battle one another with more than a hundred water balloons, leaving in their wake the exploded, colorful plastic pieces, all of which then had to be picked out of the grass.

Rich and I had our own Nantucket rituals. Once Michael went to sleep at night, we enjoyed the rare pleasure of sitting in the yard, staring at the night sky, listening to the quiet, and sipping wine.

Nantucket held a trove of potential pets. From the time Michael was four until he was about ten or eleven, every day at the beach, he would capture jellyfish, sand crabs, and sea lice, put them in a bucket, and insist that he wanted to bring them back to the cottage and then back to New York. Initially, Rich and I did not react to Michael's desires in the same way. I was always trying to figure out how to say no without seeming like the exhausted mother I was. Rich was always trying to figure out how this could be made to work. Rich's undaunted spirit always prevailed.

Every summer, the backyard was lined with buckets and bottles of all shapes and sizes. Fortunately, the sea creatures never lived long enough to make the trip back to New York, but they did live long enough in their buckets to overpower the sweet scent of honeysuckle that grew wild in the backyard.

ı ı ı

The collection, care, and feeding of all these sea creatures made Rich and me realize we were on the road to buying Michael some kind of pet. A dog was still out of the question; that had definitely not changed. But right before Michael started kindergarten, right after Inchie died, once we were back in the city, we bought fish. Goldfish. Three of them: "Beautiful," "Goldie," and "Blackie." Goldie died first. Blackie was soon to follow. I wondered if maybe we could prolong Beautiful's life by feeding it less. I nearly starved the fish, but, remarkably, it went on to live with us for years.

On Michael's first day of kindergarten, he drew a family portrait and listed the members of his family: Mom, Dad, Michael, and Beautiful. I noticed the other kids had lists that looked more like, Mom, Dad, Susie, Joey, Sarah, and Fido.

Michael was an only child of older parents, and although that provided him with a kind of closeness to his parents he might otherwise not have had, it also meant he didn't have siblings to play with, fight with, and make fun of his parents with. He also didn't have a dog. He had Beautiful.

We bought him more fish. After buying, starving, and burying many more fish, we finally retired the tank. Unable to hold and pet the fish, not to mention their rapid demise, Michael's interest in the fish had naturally waned, though his interest in pets and animals in general had not. If anything, Rich and I had frustrated him by never allowing him a pet he could really play with.

Every so often, Michael would wear me down with a steady stream of comments like "I just need a dog to love," or "If I had a dog I'd always have a friend." I'd start to ruminate again about getting a dog. But I knew that even if I could see my way clear, Rich could not. He was willing to take on the overseeing of goldfish, but I knew he would protest at the expense and responsibility of adding a dog to our already demanding lives.

Rich was running his own consulting business; I was always at the newspaper or on the phone with someone there. There wasn't time for a dog. On a couple of occasions I started to broach the subject, but Rich never really wanted to get too far into it, ending the conversation with: "Can we talk about this some other time?"

Which really meant: "I haven't changed my mind, and I don't want to talk about it."

On occasion, though, Rich would start to grapple with getting Michael a pet that required more of a commitment on our part than fish. When Michael was in fourth grade, Rich and I took him to East Hill Farm, a working farm in Massachusetts. After collecting eggs, riding a horse, and learning how to milk a cow, Michael discovered the baby rabbits. He spent every waking moment attending to them. Rich started musing about owning a rabbit. "At least," he said, "it is an animal that would not have to be walked." But if it was unthinkable to own a dog, it was utter insanity to think about bringing a rabbit into a New York City apartment.

Michael continued to long for a dog, and we continued to say no and to surround him with poor substitutes. One year, Santa brought Michael a kit that allowed him to hatch butterflies. We sent away for the cocoons, watched and waited until they magically turned into butterflies, and then struggled with whether or not to let them go.

We hit a real low point when Michael came home from school one day and announced that a neighborhood friend's rat was about to have babies and his buddy had offered to give Michael one. "He said I could have one of the babies. Isn't that great?" Michael said to me, smiling ear to ear.

I had to call the boy's mother and ask her to please not allow her child to give Michael a rat. She didn't see why I was so distraught. I asked her what she would do if Michael had tempted her son with a new puppy, one of the few pets her son did not own. Six months later, I saw the mother and her son walking their new dog.

It was around that time that one of Michael's friends and fellow New York Yankees devotees, Jack Schlossberg, a boy with two sisters and no brothers, got a dog: "August Yankee Alfonso Soriano Schlossberg." Jack was so in love with August that he referred to him as his brother. Jack's mother had been one of the dog holdouts. She had once gone so far as to caution me that if I ever felt myself weakening, I should call her and she'd set me straight. When she called to say she had weakened, her first words were: "I know you're going to kill me, but . . ."

Many of our New York friends had also wrestled with the dog issue and decided against it, saying, too, that the complications of life in the city just made the prospect daunting. There was something ironic about the whole mind-set. Here we were, all making sacrifices so that our children could have every advantage in life. We managed to keep a hundred balls in the air all the time, and yet we just couldn't see our way to taking care of a dog.

One friend, Susan Finkelstein, the mother of Jesse,

another of Michael's friends, repeatedly quoted to me what a friend of hers had said: "It just may be the one thing all of our kids are going to have to do without."

But it became harder and harder as Michael got older. Like most kids, he had no idea what taking care of a dog would actually be like—walking, bathing, feeding—and he'd vow in the most earnest and heart-breaking way that he would happily take on all of the responsibilities himself. "I promise I will walk him if you come with me, and I will feed him, and he can sleep in my room, if we can just get a dog for me to play with," he'd say. The longing was genuine. He was simply desperate.

Nothing would set Michael off like seeing a dog, especially "Rocket," a shy, auburn-colored toy poodle who was the newest member of the Simon family, neighbors who lived three floors above us in an identical apartment, with an only child, too. Emily was two years younger than Michael. She was the sweet, composed, adored daughter of Jennifer and Paul.

Of all the dogs Michael had ever fallen in love with, none captured his heart the way Rocket did, not even McDuff. After all, Rocket lived in our building, not in the pages of a book. One frigid winter's day, we saw Rocket dressed in a red sweater and Michael declared him "the cutest, most adorable dog I have ever seen in my entire life." It was another of those moments when I

walked right up to the edge of relenting before backing away.

| | |

By the time Michael was eleven, his life was chockablock with school, friends, and baseball. Over spring break, for the first time in his life, we were headed to Europe. Michael had not brought up the dog subject for a while.

I, however, thinking I had an opportunity to add a convincing point to the ongoing debate, did something foolishly daring. I proclaimed, "We wouldn't be able to take a vacation like this if we had a dog."

As usual, Michael was prepared. "I've already talked to Auntie Babs, and she said anytime we went away, she'd take care of my dog. Please, Mom, please, can we get a dog? I will never ask for anything else. I promise!"

My younger sister, Barbara Clark (Auntie Babs), and her husband, Dave, and their three children live in Ramsey, New Jersey, in a house with a fenced-in yard. The Clarks have owned many dogs. They were in fact what one might call "dog people." It was too perfect. I was cooked. Backed into a corner of my own making, I actually found myself desperately declaring, "We can talk about it when you're older." I now hated myself.

We had a glorious trip—Rome, Florence, and Venice.

Michael was now old enough to read the guidebooks, tote his own suitcase, figure out what he wanted to order in a restaurant, and appreciate the more civilized pace of life in a Mediterranean country.

While climbing the 463 steep, narrow, winding steps in Brunelleschi's Dome in Florence, the family backpack stuffed with water bottles, jackets, books, and souvenirs became too cumbersome for Rich, age fifty-six and the recipient of two artificial hip joints. Michael happily and gallantly offered to carry it on his own back. A line was crossed. Michael was growing up faster than I realized and probably faster than I was ready for. It is a funny thing about parenting: by the time you get used to understanding and dealing with one age, your child has already moved on to the next.

Toward the end of the trip, as we sat at Caffè Quadri, an outdoor café in San Marco Square in Venice, basking in the sun's warmth, watching Michael tirelessly feeding the pigeons, something happened that made me think more seriously than I ever had about getting Michael a dog.

Michael had spent so much time feeding the pigeons that we had spent $70 on food for them. But it wasn't the money spent on pigeon feed that made me see the dog situation differently; it was two teenage boys who were making sport of tormenting the birds. The boys had lured the birds with feed, captured them, and started pulling their wings. One of the boys acted as though he was going to twist one of the birds' heads off. It was a horrible scene. Michael was overwrought. "Dad, make them stop! You have to make them stop!" he cried.

That was the exact moment I secretly started to seriously abandon my long-held position on owning a dog. It was an epiphany. Michael had to have a dog. How could I ignore my son's love for animals, which had only deepened throughout his childhood? Why wasn't I listening to him when he said he "needed" a dog? He really was getting older. Maybe he could take on some of the responsibilities. Maybe we could make this work. Why was I so willing to spend money on everything else for him except a dog?

Maybe I wanted to hold on to my son's childhood, or maybe I had some sixth sense of what I was about to learn was on our family's road ahead. But I sat there watching Michael with the pigeons and put aside my own limitations to think seriously about Michael's unquestionable, unabated love of God's creatures. I vowed to myself I would once again raise the subject with Rich as soon as the time seemed right.

The time came soon.

Chapter 2

I ARRIVED AT THE radiologist's office four days after our return from Italy. There were no other patients in the waiting room. The receptionist called me over and asked a few questions. "No, my address has not changed." "Yes, my insurance is the same." "Yes, I understand that I have to pay today for the services rendered today." "Yes, I have been here before." "Yes, I do want to actually see the doctor and not have my test results mailed."

While we were away I had managed to forget about my work, a rarity for me, but I could never manage to fully shake the nagging dread that when we returned home to New York, I had to get a mammogram. I was overdue.

I hated those checkups—the anxiety; the chilly, sterile environment; sitting around braless in a cheap, flimsy gown; the endless, endless waiting. I hated staring at all the other women who were waiting, too—all of them trying to make small talk and avoid it at the same time. I thought if I took the first appointment of the day, there would be less waiting. I was wrong.

I sat there that cold, rainy, Monday morning in March leafing through the well-thumbed magazines. No *Times* or *Newsweeks* here; it was either magazines full of recipes or ones with ideas for reigniting a decades-old marriage. If the magazines aren't interesting enough, there are the pamphlets about breast cancer. My "favorite" had a picture of a breast with a rainbow going through it. The walls are pink. In fact, there is a lot of pink there, the color of little girls. There is something demeaning about all that pink. Cancer is not pink. Cancer is serious business.

No one thought to pipe in music, so every sound—every clearing of the throat, sneeze, page turn, zip of a handbag—was magnified. It was becoming crowded. Ten women, mostly in their fifties and sixties, were all wearing the same expression: worry.

I thought about how earlier that morning I had hugged Michael, sent him off to school, and watched him walk away. *That's the last time I'll hug him without knowing I have breast cancer,* I thought. I instantly scolded myself, *You are really, really crazy.* Some years ago, when I hit forty, a friend told me that we were now at the age when every headache is a brain tumor. I put my paranoia about breast cancer in the "headache is a brain tumor" category and headed toward the doctor's office. After all, this was just a routine mammogram.

It was always the same. The technician would squeeze one of my breasts between two steel plates, tell me not to breathe, disappear behind a wall, and take the x-ray. Then she would do the same thing to the other breast. I'd be dismissed and sent to another waiting room. Sometimes I would be called back for reasons no clearer than, "We need another picture."

I sat there at 9:00 that morning, in my pink gown, growing more and more anxious. The technician said they needed another picture. Back again. Don't breathe. Have a seat outside. Another waiting room. More magazines. There was no source of natural light in the inner waiting room; I felt the walls closing in. The more I tried to persuade myself that the long wait had nothing to do with the results of my mammogram, the more I thought the long wait meant I was that one in seven women who would be handed a diagnosis of breast cancer.

And then, after the endless wait for the new picture to be developed, the doctor saw me.

Her office was dark, lighted mostly by an illuminated screen that held the x-rays of my breasts. My regular doctor was away, so this much younger woman, with a stern and determined demeanor, was filling in.

She was thin and had long blond hair. She did not look friendly or approachable in any way. One might call her "plain." She was probably ten years my junior. Before she spoke a word, I knew something was wrong.

"There is something suspicious on the x-ray," she said, as she pointed to a mass that looked indistinguishable to me from the other masses on the film.

I didn't panic. I had a twisted sense of relief in just being out of the waiting room and finally in front of a doctor, someone who could end the unknowing. I'm also pretty good at steeling myself in a moment of crisis. The journalist often takes over and starts asking a lot of questions, listening for the nuance in the answers, trying to detect information not intended to be divulged. As long as I'm still reporting the story, gathering facts and not writing the story, there is no conclusion, no bad ending. Anything is still possible. It is usually later that I fall apart.

"When was your last mammogram?" she asked. Without waiting for the answer, she said, "You should have a sonogram as soon as possible."

"Can it be done now?" I asked. Fortunately, "now" was possible. I didn't have to make another appointment for another day and wait some more. Waiting had already become excruciating.

The medical suite had two floors. The sonogram machine was down a narrow, winding staircase. Another waiting room. More magazines. More waiting. More women sitting around braless in cheap, pink gowns trying not to notice one another. No one was there with a husband or a companion of any kind. Each of the women in the waiting room was alone.

I was called to the examining room. I took my place on the cold metal table. I lay there remembering the only other time in my life I had any kind of sonogram. I was pregnant, my husband was holding my hand, and we were ecstatic to see our son, sucking his thumb and floating around in amniotic fluid.

I started thinking, too, about the day Michael was born. It was also a Monday morning. Michael was born at 9:01 on a crystal-clear, perfect, sparkling spring day in early May. There wasn't a cloud in the sky. I had always been told that first babies arrived late. Michael was two weeks early. I was fully dilated by the time we got to the hospital. There wasn't time to fill out admissions papers, and I was way past the point of any discussion of epidural drugs.

Before I knew it, I was whisked to a delivery room and Michael came charging into the world. Rich watched as the doctor cut the umbilical cord and placed Michael in my arms. I kissed his small cheeks, and his nose and the top of his head and then his hands and his feet. I stared into his eyes. To me, he was a miracle and I could not take my eyes off him. I had loved him from the second I knew I was pregnant.

It was a day of unbridled joy. My sister Barbara, having ditched work, arrived with a bouquet of yellow tulips and purple irises. She was the first of my siblings to get to the hospital, the first to hold the newborn nephew.

The cold gel on my breast startled me, ending my reverie. "We'll look at the left breast first." The technician was as humorless as the doctor had been. Their inability to make even the most superficial human connection with me made me feel even more alone than I was. I thought they wanted no part of me, as though I had some fatal, communicable disease. There were no niceties, no putting the patient at ease. It was all business. No one seemed to have any sense that psychic relief would go a long way to bringing down the emotional temperature of all those women in the waiting room, not to mention me, lying on the steel table with cold gel on my breast looking for clues in their remote expressions.

It was dark in this room, too. The doctor came in and repeated much of what the technician had already done, looking at a screen while she moved a probe across one breast and then the other. The sonogram confirmed what the mammogram had shown: a mass in my left breast with the distinctive shape of a cancerous breast tumor. The doctor said, "Yes, that's just what I thought." She seemed almost self-congratulatory, pleased she had gotten it right. She was oblivious to the forty-eight-year-old woman lying on the table, one step closer to a diagnosis of breast cancer.

I asked what the chances were that the mass was cancer. The doctor answered, "I'm going to be honest" (as if there were another option). "There is a 75 percent chance that it is malignant. We'll need a biopsy to be sure."

I said I wanted it done that day. I didn't care how long I had to wait. Fortunately, whoever had a biopsy scheduled for that dreary morning had canceled. The machinery and the staff were available. I could have the biopsy done right then and there.

The doctor asked if I wanted to call someone. She didn't say, "You might be a little uncomfortable. Do you want to call someone to pick you up in case you'd like help getting home?" Not even "Do you want to call and let someone know what's going on?" Just "Do you want to call someone?" I felt like a prisoner making my one allotted phone call.

Rich was so cheerful when he answered the phone. "Hi, sweetie, everything go all right this morning? I was beginning to worry when I hadn't heard from you."

Rich and I had been married for twenty years. I knew that no matter what I said next, or what tone of voice I used, he would know that something was seriously wrong. I could have said I was fine and he would have known that I was not.

I wanted to stay on the phone with Rich and hurry

him off at the same time. "I'm still in the doctor's office. They found something," I managed to say without crying. "I have to have another test. Can you come right over?"

I kept staring down at my shoes, fixing my eyes on something so I would not get dizzy and fall. They were the same shoes I had on just days earlier, sitting at Caffè Quadri, where Rich and I had sat enjoying the sun's warmth and watching Michael feed pigeons. Our waiter, Nicolai, had spun stories for us about life in Venice and was as content as we were to have us linger for hours over a cappuccino.

"I'll be right there." Rich knew to just come and not ask me any questions.

There was a flurry of paper signing, absolving the doctor if anything went wrong. The procedure was called a core biopsy and involved taking five specimens. For the first time all morning, there was no waiting. I did not have a chance to see Rich, to have him hold me before being summoned for the biopsy.

I lay down on the same steel table I had been on for the sonogram. The doctor used the sonogram to guide the needles one after the other into my breast and into the suspicious mass where cells were withdrawn for analysis. There was an instrument that looked like a gun, and it made a popping noise each time the cells were withdrawn. I looked away.

I wasn't scared. I didn't feel like crying. I didn't mind

the pain. I was still reporting the story, still fact gathering. I was keeping my emotions at bay. In that moment, I tried not to think about Rich or Michael. I tried not to think about the fact that Michael was only eleven years old. I tried not to think about the devastating effects a parent's deteriorating health can have on a child, how it can rob them of innocence and make them grow up too soon, something I knew firsthand. Instead, I focused on whom I knew who could help me find the right doctors, the best care. I started making mental lists of the people I could turn to for help.

At the same time, I was growing impatient with the detached, morose mood of the doctor and the technician. These were clearly people who had spent too much time with machines. If I had relied on their demeanor to give me insight into my own situation, I probably would have assumed I was near death. When she was about to insert the fifth needle into my breast, the doctor finally had a rare human moment and asked if I was "all right."

The biopsy was over quickly. Three hours after I had first put on the shabby pink gown, I was told to get dressed. The doctor said she would know the results of the biopsy in three days and I could call her at four o'clock on Thursday—just what I was hoping for, more waiting.

I got dressed, thinking only about what I could do

to get more information. But when I went up the stairs to pay my bill and saw Rich sitting by the desk, my detached journalist mode gave way and I wanted to cry. But I didn't. I paid my $1,500 bill with Rich standing next to me. He took my hand and we left the office.

Once the elevator doors closed, Rich took me in his arms and said "I love you," as he held me tight. "Whatever it is, we'll get through it. I promise."

And then, finally, we walked out into the cool, moist afternoon air.

I met Rich Pinsky when I was twenty-three years old and he was thirty-one. I had now known him for more years of my life than I had not known him. We met while working temporary jobs at a social service agency, each of us on our way to writing careers. My memory is that Rich said something to me about my smile; his memory is that I updated him on that day's political news, that Jimmy Carter had appointed Edmund Muskie secretary of state.

Neither of us had any money then. We spent a lot of time getting to know each other on a tight budget—walking through Central Park, sitting in coffee shops, wandering around the Metropolitan Museum of Art, and taking the PATH train to Hoboken, New Jersey, where at night you could sit and look across the Hudson River at the glittering Manhattan skyline.

In the years we had been married, we had our share

of trials—my father's death, Rich's hip replacement surgery, periods of financial struggle, the death of close friends. But we had never faced a health matter that threatened to take one of us from the other.

There was not much to do at this point but pray. We walked home, hand in hand. I explained to Rich about the morose doctor and the sonogram and the needle that made a popping sound. I told him I really had no information beyond the doctor saying that she thinks the mass she saw is likely to be cancerous. He reacted the way I did—he pushed his emotions to some far corner of his heart. "Let's wait and see," he said. "Let's wait until we know what if anything we are dealing with and then we'll figure out how to proceed."

We stopped by my local church, St. Ignatius Loyola. We slipped in through a side door of the Roman basilica-like church and walked down a long aisle, past the baptismal font and depictions of the first seven Stations of the Cross, to a small altar. I lit a candle and prayed for strength. I don't know if I felt the closeness of God or the closeness of childhood, but I felt calmed.

I sat down in a pew with Rich beside me and I thought about my childhood, the happiest days of which were spent in Fairfield, Connecticut, where I lived with my parents, two sisters, a brother, and a dog in a white colonial house on a dead-end street with a brook at one end and a hill at the other. At the top of the hill, a stone fence and two white boulders marked the divide between our street and the property of an adjacent country club. When I asked my father why we didn't belong to the country club, he told me it was because "Clubs are designed to keep people out, and I don't think that's something we'd want to be a part of."

It was a close-knit neighborhood. On hot summer nights, the kids on the block stayed outside playing kick-ball in the middle of the street until it was so dark we could no longer see the ball. We went sled riding and ice-skating in the winter. In spring, we rode our bicycles down the hill, daring each other to do it without holding on to the handlebars and without falling off at a spot where tree roots pushed through the concrete.

My sister Barbara and I used to play "train" on the winding steps leading to the attic bedrooms. Barbara had been given some toy suitcases one Christmas. We'd pack them full of our dolls' clothes, take the luggage and the dolls, and board the train. Our imaginations took us all over the world to places we had only heard of but never been—Paris, Rome, and New Haven.

Another of our favorite games was "school," with each of us having a classroom full of imaginary students. Our older sister, Louise, had beautifully illustrated fairy-tale books. We'd pile into her bed, and she'd read to us. Our brother, Bill, collected baseball cards and taught us how to play a game where you would stand the cards against the floor molding and flick others to knock them down.

During my grade-school years, my two best friends were Betsey Weldon, who lived next door, and Mary Beth Quinn, who lived at the end of the block. We'd sleep over at one another's house. Often, when it was my turn to sleep at Betsey's or Mary Beth's, darkness would fall and I'd decide that life was really better back at my own house. The unfamiliar, creaking floors, the shadows on the walls, the intimidating parents in the next room, all made me long for the comfort of my own room and my own bed.

I'd sneak out of bed and dial 336-5148, hoping the *click, click, click* of the spinning dial would not be overheard. The voice on the other end always said the same thing: "I'll be right there." My father would come and take me and my Raggedy Ann doll and my pillow home without making me feel embarrassed about being too homesick to stay the night at someone else's house.

Mary Beth's family was the first on the block to get a color TV. She had Barbie dolls. Betsey's family had the cast album to *The Sound of Music,* and a little room in the basement stocked with cans of food in case war broke out. They ate white toast with butter and cinnamon and sugar on it. I envied them all those things.

But neither Betsey nor Mary Beth had a younger sister to boss around, or a brother who was a ham radio operator and could talk to people from all over. Through my eight-year-old eyes, they were not taken into New York City as often as we to see plays, or to have fancy dinners in restaurants where the waiter came over with a giant pepper mill. Their mothers did not play "Clair de Lune" on the piano, and I don't know if their fathers packed all the neighborhood kids into the family station wagon to take them for ice cream as often as mine did.

Everyone in the neighborhood did have a dog and we did, too. He was one of the largest on the block, a golden retriever, a birthday present for my brother, Bill, who named him "Scout."

On occasion, Scout would sneak out the back door, sending the entire neighborhood into a panic. "Scout's loose! Scout's loose!" The screams could be heard from front porches up and down the block. Sooner or later, Scout wandered home, having taken a swim in the brook or a run through the country club. Sometimes my father would take the family station wagon out, park it by the brook, and call to Scout, who sooner or later would come running. Even though the scenario was oft repeated, I was always scared when it happened. Surely the day would come when Scout would run away and not find his way home.

As adults, my siblings and I all look back on those Connecticut days as the happiest, most stable time of our childhood. Eventually my father had some shattering financial setbacks, and his heart disease went from a disease he could live with to a disease likely to kill him. He often could not work.

When he'd fall asleep in front of the television, or reading a book, or close his eyes while listening to music, I'd stare at him to see if he was still breathing. When I left for school each morning, I wondered if he'd be alive when I got home.

For all of us, life became unmoored and stayed that way for many, many years. My mother struggled single-handedly to support four kids and a sick husband. She was a nurse, though she had started her career as a research physicist. In her early twenties, she turned down the government's invitation to work on the Manhattan Project, standing firm in her belief that nuclear weapons would only lead to more war. It was a brave thing to do. She thought about becoming a doctor, but loved the world of books and characters drawn from the imagination more than she did science. She set out to teach English literature. But life circumstances and World War II led her to nursing. She helped the wounded heal body and soul. It became her life's work.

My parents' changing financial fortunes in general, and my father's search for an employer interested in hiring a man with a razor-sharp mind but declining health, caused us to move around a lot.

One of the darkest periods came during a brief move

we made to New Orleans, where my father took a job expanding a wholesale drug company based in St. Louis. It was an odd fit. The boss didn't know my father was the kind who would not join clubs. He was dismayed when my father put a television in the warehouse so the workers could watch the funeral of Martin Luther King Jr. The relationship deteriorated quickly, and so did my father's health. Now, forty years later, I can still vividly recall his gasping for air on the front porch on a thickly humid night. My father survived that episode and we moved back north, but life always seemed to teeter on the brink of catastrophe.

We moved back north in the middle of winter. I didn't understand why we could not just return to our old house in Connecticut, where life had been so safe and happy. We were headed instead for New Jersey (which, in my mind, was at least close to Connecticut), but it wasn't home. Still, I couldn't wait to get back to the part of the country that was familiar to me. I missed the landscape of my childhood, the solid maple trees with their large leaves, the slender white birch trees, rolling hills, peonies, forsythia, and the beach. My sister Barbara and I prayed for snow, though we no longer owned sleds or ice skates.

Shortly before we moved, with our house in New Orleans full of boxes and commotion, someone went out the back gate followed by Scout. He took off. We all panicked. None of the neighbors knew us; there were no friends standing on their front porches screaming, "Scout's loose!"

My father realized Scout would not know how to get back to our house on his own, since we had lived there for such a short time and the terrain was still unfamiliar. My father combed the neighborhood for days looking for him. But his effort was for naught. He was unable to find our beloved dog. We had to move, leaving Scout behind. The pain was searing.

On the day we moved, one of the last items to be loaded onto the truck was a mirror that had hung in the entrance hall in our house in Connecticut. "I'll get it," I volunteered. "You better wait for me," my father said. "It's too heavy for you." I was then about twelve or thirteen years old; I thought he was wrong.

I wanted to surprise him and show him I could do it. I also wanted to spare him any unnecessary labor because of his heart. When the mirror slipped through my hands and shattered into hundreds of pieces on the floor, I was devastated. I was disappointed in myself, upset that I'd done something my father asked me not to. I thought I was surely in for seven years of bad luck.

A week later, on a bitter, dark January afternoon, the truck with all our possessions pulled up in front of our new house. It wasn't Fairfield, Connecticut, but it would do. Nightfall came early; the truck was barely

unloaded when the snow Barbara and I had been praying for started to softly fall. It did not stop for three days.
The awkwardness of starting at yet another new school
was put off. Barbara and I braved the frigid cold for
hours on end, hurling ourselves into drifts, diving to the
ground to make snow angels, packing tight snowballs
with wet mitten-clad hands.

In time, we settled into our uncertain family life.

Before we left New Orleans, my father had put an
ad in the newspaper offering a reward for anyone who
could help us find Scout. Days after we arrived in New
Jersey, someone called and said the man who lived next
door to her had found Scout and was keeping him. My
father hired a lawyer to get Scout back. Eventually,
Scout made it to our new home. He arrived months
after we did. Finally having him home, we all loved him
more than ever, but he was no longer in good health,
and he died soon after.

Despite the turbulence of those years, or maybe because of it, my sisters, my brother, and I learned to stick
together. In a crisis, there would be no question about
whether we would all show up. The only question would
be who would get there first.

But sitting in that church pew with Rich, I didn't
want to tell them or my eighty-three-year-old mother
that I might have breast cancer. I also did not want to
tell any of our friends that Rich and I were waiting for

potentially life-altering news. They were all waiting to hear about our fabulous holiday in Italy.

I thought about the struggles and sadness of my own childhood, how chaos and my father's failing health hung over so much of it, and how badly I wanted something else for Michael.

As we walked home from the church, Rich said: "You know, it is still possible that the doctor is wrong."

But I knew in my gut that the doctor was right. I think Rich knew it, too.

Rich is usually certain of his positions. He was certain Bill Clinton would defeat George H. W. Bush, even as the White House correspondent for *The Times*, our good friend Andy Rosenthal, told him how wrong-headed his thinking was. Rich was certain we'd return to Nantucket every summer, even though our finances suggested otherwise. He was certain I'd love Venice.

Rich also was certain that if the test results confirmed the cancer diagnosis, the disease would not take my life; we'd get through it intact and would only love each other more. I felt vulnerable enough that I put him in the awful position of having to tell me that several times over the next few days.

"You should try to stay home from work today," Rich said when we were finally home from the doctor's office and from our stop at the church. I considered the idea for a minute, but I knew the best thing for me was to go to work. Even if I had not been in Italy away from the paper for a couple of weeks, I knew it was better for me to sit at my desk, answer e-mails, return phone calls, gossip with my colleagues, and start putting my mind back into the vagaries of American politics than for me to sit home and tempt depression. I never appreciated the rituals of daily life more than I did at that moment.

I had to find a way to make the hours from Monday afternoon until Thursday afternoon feel like something less than eternity. I was too edgy even to sit and have a cup of coffee with Rich before leaving.

"Call me when you get to work," Rich said, as he walked me to the front door. I walked out of our apartment and toward the subway. I felt invisible. I engaged the man at the newspaper stand in a longer conversation than my usual "thank you," now asking about his family and how his children were doing in school.

I descended the concrete steps into the subway, this time in a way I don't recall ever doing before, by holding on to the cold, metal handrail for support. My train came right away. Rush hour had long passed, and there were plenty of seats, but I didn't take one. I stood, grasping one of the poles, studying the faces of my fellow passengers, particularly women, wondering if any of them had cancer.

Once I was safely inside *The Times*, I sat down at my desk and did what any journalist would: I started researching breast cancer. I put off returning e-mails and phone calls. I typed "breast cancer survival rates" into Google. One million, one hundred thirty thousand citations appeared.

Newsrooms are full of people protecting secrets. Usually the secrets have to do with who was willing or not willing to go on the record about a public official's wrongdoing or about some corporation that's been making gazillions in some questionable way or about an athlete who isn't quite as superhuman as his fans have come to think. The burden of carrying the secret is shared between reporter and editor, and sometimes a wider circle than that. But my secret was about me, and I wasn't ready to share it with anyone. The burden of carrying it for now was mine alone.

Still, there was comfort at work, in the familiar banter of colleagues I had worked with for decades, in the routine of the day—talking to reporters about their stories, answering e-mails, reading stories, and sitting through the afternoon meeting where decisions are made about which stories will appear on the next day's front page.

I was going to need those comforts to get me through the next few days. Rich had to go out of town on Tuesday and would not be back until Thursday, making waiting to hear from the doctor even more difficult. I'd be alone with Michael after work each day, making dinner, overseeing homework, getting him to bed each night. I would have to put all my worries about cancer out of my mind. There are no better readers of people than kids. If I was going to keep my secret from Michael, I was going to have to work at it.

I tried to keep my mind occupied with work and Michael's life. Each night, I made one of Michael's favorite dinners: spaghetti and meatballs, macaroni and cheese, or salmon. And each night I went to bed shortly after him, at around 9:30, so I would not have to lie in bed awake and alone in the dark thinking about cancer. I was less fearful about being awake and alone too early in the morning, when it was at least light out and I'd be able to busy myself with reading the morning papers, than I was about being awake and alone at night, prey to fear. I could have used the comfort of a dog.

After breakfast each of those mornings, Michael and I would board the crosstown bus for the west side, where Michael goes to school. I'd walk him to the school's front door and then take the subway down to Times Square to my job at the newspaper. I always liked taking Michael to school; it was a rare opportunity to just sit on the bus together and talk for a while.

Thursday finally came. I left work early in order to make the call to the doctor in the privacy of my bedroom. When I arrived home, Michael and his babysitter, Caroline Clarke, were sitting at the dining room table playing Stratego, one of their favorite board games. "Hi Mom," Michael called when he heard me come in. "I'm winning," he said as he and Caroline continued moving their red and blue armies around the board trying to avoid setting off bombs.

Rich had said he'd do everything he could to be home by the time I called the doctor. But it was getting late, and I could not wait and risk calling after office hours only to find the doctor had gone.

I went into my room, closed the door, pulled a reporter's notebook out of a drawer, paced for a moment, and then sat down at the desk. I reached for the phone and dialed the number of the doctor's office that I had written on a piece of paper earlier in the day and put in my pocket. I was calm. I asked for the doctor, saying she was expecting my call. "Hold on," was the anonymous reply at the other end. I was kept on "hold" for ten excruciating minutes. "She's busy right now and said your results have not yet come in and you should call back tomorrow."

"But the doctor told me explicitly that she would have the results by now. Can you ask her to call the lab and get the results? I really can't wait any longer." Again I was told to hold on.

In a matter of seconds, the doctor got on the phone and said: "I do have your results, Ms. Elder; you do have invasive, lobular breast cancer. You should get in touch with your gynecologist, who will be able to recommend a surgeon."

Just then Rich walked into our bedroom. I managed to ask the doctor, "Based on the lab report, what else can you tell me about the cancer?" She said: "It is slow growing, but the tumor is large. You will need surgery, chemotherapy, and radiation."

And with that, she hung up the phone.

CHAPTER 3

"**H**ONEY, we have to get Michael a dog."
Minutes after I hung up the phone with the doctor and told Rich what she had said, I was the one who was pleading. The diagnosis of cancer had brought a sense of urgency to my life. Michael's emotional need for a dog was now unequivocal. I wanted to give him the dog he imagined in that PowerPoint presentation so many years ago—the one that will "give you a hug when you feel sad."

My cancer treatments were going to be a long, hard road for us all—surgery, months of chemotherapy, radiation. I wanted us to promise Michael that at the end of all this sadness, he'd have his dog. I didn't want Michael to lose any of his innocence or buoyancy or sweetness or faith in the goodness and promise of life. I didn't want him to spend the next six months worrying about

me, overhearing conversations with words in them like *survival* and *depressed immune system*; I wanted him to spend those months excited about getting a dog.

"Okay, okay, we can talk about it," Rich said.

"We have to do this," I said. "Michael has been right all along. He does need a dog, and now he needs a dog more than ever. What better antidote to all this worry and gloom than the anticipation of a puppy?"

And then I realized that both Michael and Rich could be in for an emotional maelstrom. "We don't know what is going to happen to me," I said in a voice as devoid of sentiment as I could manage. "If I get worse instead of better, a dog will help Michael and maybe you, too."

Rich asked the obvious but reasonable questions: How much will this cost? Who is going to train this dog? and How were we going to manage it all? He said he knew right then and there that the dog walking would fall to him.

"No, it won't, really," I said. Reminding him of what our neighbors with the toy poodle had told us, I said: "Jennifer told me you can paper-train these small dogs." Then, to bolster my case, I added: "The walking isn't really a problem. I can do it in the morning and at night. Caroline can do it in the afternoon."

My pitch to Rich was starting to sound eerily like the one Michael had been making to me for so many years. I tried to explain that all this would eventually become Michael's responsibility, just as soon as he was old enough to go out unsupervised on New York City streets. Rich was not persuaded. He gave in anyway.

Once the decision was made, Rich, typically, was fully onboard, though he had one stipulation: "It has to look like a boy's dog. I don't want us to get one of those small white dogs that looks like a woman's slipper, or looks like it belongs to a girl," he declared. "If it's going to be a small dog, let's at least get one that's a dark color, like black."

I decided to resist my usual urge to jump all over Rich for what I considered an utterly ridiculous remark. What about the legions of women in New York whose entire wardrobes are black, I wanted to say. Never mind. He had agreed to a dog, and I was thrilled.

Rich and I also agreed that the puppy couldn't arrive just yet. Although we had not yet lined up a team of cancer doctors and were still operating in the dark, we knew enough to realize that having a new puppy in the house would have to wait until the treatments were completed. The chemotherapy would make me sick a lot of the time, the radiation would deplete my physical energy. For now it would be enough for Michael just to know his prayers had been answered. For me, just thinking about getting the dog for Michael was already giving me comfort.

It was going to be good for us all to have a puppy, a new life at the center of our lives, a declaration of faith in the future. Michael was older now, and I was less worried about leaving him asleep in the apartment alone if Rich were away and I had to walk the dog at night. Auntie Babs could take care of the dog when we went away. We could do this. We had to.

Rich and I decided to tell Michael on his twelfth birthday, May 10, that he would finally have the puppy he had wanted for so long. Although we wouldn't be able to get the dog until the fall, the sooner he knew about the dog, the sooner he and we would have something to distract us from cancer.

By sheer coincidence, May 10 was also the day we were scheduled to get the postsurgery pathology report. You cannot know the extent cancer has invaded your body until you get that report. Once I had it, I would know how far the cancer had spread, how many lymph nodes were involved, whether or not I was a candidate for some of the newer drugs that offered promise for long-term survival. A friend who had been treated for breast cancer cautioned me that the week of waiting for the pathology report can be psychologically debilitating. In fact, her exact words were "It will be the worst week of your life."

It *was* the worst week of my life. The salve was plotting and planning how Rich and I would tell Michael he was finally going to get a dog. We could say it outright, or we could give him some telltale gifts, like a leash, or a bowl, or a doggie bed. We decided instead to make a poster with a picture of a small dog. That way, he'd have both a keepsake of the moment and also a minute to take it all in. And we'd have the unparalleled joy of seeing Michael's face when he realized he was about to get a real, living, breathing dog of his own, the pet he had ached for most of his life.

A few days before Michael's birthday, while Michael was out of the house, Rich went into Michael's room to use Michael's computer, which was attached to our color printer, to print out the announcement he had made:

HAPPY BIRTHDAY, MICHAEL!
FOR YOUR BIRTHDAY, YOU WILL BE GETTING A PUPPY
OF YOUR VERY OWN. START THINKING OF NAMES
AND MAKING A PLACE IN YOUR ROOM FOR HIS BED.
WE LOVE YOU,
MOM AND DAD

Below the note was a picture of a black toy poodle, sitting on a sun-drenched lawn, looking straight at the camera, with a tennis ball in front of him. Like Rocket, this toy poodle had a "puppy cut," rather than a "poodle cut," which made him look more like a shaggy dog than a poodle, more American than, well, French.

While Rich was busy with the poster I went out to try to find a tiny stuffed black dog that at least resembled the one we had in mind to accompany the announcement. I walked to a nearby toy store, about fifteen blocks from where we lived (a reasonable walk by New York standards). I found just the right little stuffed dog.

It was a lot more fun thinking about how surprised Michael was going to be in a few days when he opened the poster than thinking about that pathology report.

Little did we know, however, that our carefully plotted surprise would be thwarted by a simple oversight. While I was at the store Michael had come home from school and sat down at his computer to do homework. Microsoft Word, the program he uses, and the one from which Rich had printed the poster, keeps track of the names of the last several documents the computer user has worked on, even if the file was never saved on that computer. Sitting at his desk, staring at his computer screen, Michael looked for his history notes and saw the list of the most recently retrieved documents. There, at the top of the list: MIKE'S BDAY DOG. He was flabbergasted.

For a moment, Michael just sat there, staring at the words. He hesitated before mentioning what he had seen. But, as he would later say, the thought of his own dog soon "crowded out" all other thoughts in his head. He got up so quickly from his chair, he nearly knocked it to the ground.

"Dad! Dad! Dad!" he called, as he burst through the door of the room where Rich was working. "Is it really true? I know I wasn't supposed to see it, but I couldn't help it. Is it really true? Am I getting a dog?"

At first Rich could not figure out how Michael could possibly have divined that his prayers had been answered. And then Michael explained, "Dad, I know I'm not supposed to know, but I turned on my computer and saw . . ."

"Oh, Mikey, we wanted to tell you on your birthday. I printed our letter to you off your computer and I forgot to erase the evidence," Rich said as he got up from his chair. "Yes, honey, you are getting a dog, just as soon as Mom's treatments are over."

Michael ran to Rich, threw his arms around him, jumping up and down, shouting: "I can't believe it! I can't believe it!"

I walked in the front door soon after. Michael, hearing my key in the lock, flung the door open before I had a chance to turn the key. "Thank you, Mom, thank you so much," he said, grabbing me around the waist and hugging me. "I can't believe this is finally happening. I can't believe I am going to have a dog."

Rich followed close behind Michael, explaining what had happened and how it was that Michael had come to know that his dream of owning a dog would be realized.

The next day at school, Michael told all of his buddies and his teachers that at long last he would be getting a dog. "They were so happy for me," he reported back.

ı ı ı

The elation lasted. It swept us all through the beginning of my chemotherapy treatments in June, and into the summer months. Michael went away to camp for most of July. His letters home were filled with reports of baseball games won and lost, new friends made, and how he could not wait to have his new dog in the fall.

By the time we picked Michael up at the end of the month, chemotherapy had left me bald. The first thing he asked when he got into the car was if I would take off my scarf so he could see and touch my head.

"That is so cool," he said as he ran his fingers across the top of my head. Michael seemed completely unfazed.

I had bought a wig in advance of going bald. I didn't realize until I was actually facing my bald self in a mirror that I just wasn't someone who could wear a wig. There was no pretending I had hair.

Fortunately, I didn't need to wear hair to work. Some women feel their workplace demands it. I did not. Still, one of the toughest days for me was the day in late June when I walked into the newsroom of *The New York*

Times, bald. I walked into the building, past the security guard, and got into an empty elevator. I pushed 3. Our newsroom was still on Forty-third Street then, and the elevator doors had a mirrorlike finish. People were forever trying to look at themselves discreetly behind the closed doors, sucking in their stomachs, or straightening their ties. More than one woman was caught with a hairbrush or lipstick in hand. Now I was there alone, staring at a bald stranger dressed in a blue-and-white summer skirt and blue blouse, wearing a ridiculously expensive silk headscarf.

I didn't have time for a deep breath. The elevator doors opened and there stood my boss, Bill Keller, the paper's executive editor. He looked up from the stack of papers he was reading, looked at me over his half glasses and said: "Hey, Janet, how are you?"

I blurted something out about how self-conscious I felt at that moment, and how apprehensive I was about walking into the newsroom without hair. "You know," he said, "I think you look great. It only took me a few seconds to get used to seeing you this way, and that's what it will be for everyone else."

It was an extraordinarily sensitive remark. I took a deep breath and walked through the newsroom. Like most things we fear in life, the reality wasn't so bad.

No one seemed to flinch at my bald state except me. Adam Nagourney, a friend and colleague who works in Washington, had been sending me constant e-mails throughout my treatments. Shortly after I sat down at my desk that day, one arrived.

"How are things?" came across the transom that day in June. "I lost so much hair I had to have my head shaved. I'm bald," I sent back. Within seconds, Adam's response landed in my in-box. "AWESOME!" I laughed out loud.

A week after Michael came home from camp, we made our annual August sojourn to Nantucket. The air, the sun, the water were all restorative. Midway through our vacation, I left Rich and Michael on the island and I returned to New York for a couple of days to have a chemotherapy treatment. It was the sixth treatment, only two more to go, followed by six weeks of radiation. My sister Louise came with me for the hours-long session and then spent the night. She is a gentle soul and made the disruption to my relaxing beach vacation seamless.

During the months and months I underwent cancer treatments, I went to work as often as I could. When I was home, Rich tried to take time from his work, too, and we took long walks in nearby Carl Schurz Park. Being outside always made me feel better, no matter what the weather was like. It also gave us plenty of opportunity to dog watch and get a sense of different breeds.

Carl Schurz Park, home to Gracie Mansion, where New York City's mayors usually live, is up against the East River. It is one of New York's hidden treasures. The park is small, with an active corps of volunteers who hold a neighborhood tree lighting and caroling event at Christmastime and tend to its bright yellow daffodils and purple irises in the spring and its cosmos and black-eyed Susans in summer. Just when the heat is beginning to feel as though it has run its course, volunteers erect a giant movie screen on the roller hockey rink for a crowd overflowing onto the basketball court and, as night falls, show classic movies, like *Annie Hall* and *Mr. Smith Goes to Washington.* All kinds of people show up: babies asleep in their carriages and their exhausted parents, older people in need of company, teens looking for a night out, and dog owners who arrive with their dogs.

In fact, the park is seemingly always filled with people walking dogs along the promenade that runs next to the river. By fall, Rich and I were stopping people who had dogs of a certain type at the end of the leash—ones with moxie or that seemed especially sweet or playful.

Rich was by now so enthusiastic about getting a dog for Michael that he didn't hesitate to approach strangers to ask about their dogs. We developed a list: beagles, Cotons, Labradoodles, spaniels, Westies, cockapoos. They were all under consideration.

In this endless parade of dogs, it was hard to miss how well cared for they were, and how beloved they were to their owners. The dogs we met in the park were just as likely to be companions for people living alone, widows, and widowers, as they were for bustling families with children. We met a number of young couples yet unable to commit to each other but who nonetheless, together, had committed to a dog. Some dogs sat right up on the benches alongside their owners watching the boats go by on the river.

Rich and I would go home and tell Michael and Caroline about the wonderful dogs we had just met.

ɪ ɪ ɪ

I thought surely Michael would want a Westie. But, in the end, the decision was easy. He told us he wanted a toy poodle, just like Rocket, the neighbor's dog he had fallen in love with years ago and who still lived three floors above.

We dreamed of and talked animatedly and incessantly about the puppy that would join our family after the long slog of treatments for stage II breast cancer came to an end. We window-shopped in our neighborhood's many pet supply stores; Michael planned the spot in his room where his dog would sleep.

Despite my enthusiasm, a couple of times when I felt exhausted from the treatments, I started to second-guess myself about the dog. But a friend and colleague, Connie Hays, who was suffering from a form of cancer far deadlier than mine, urged me on. She had three kids and made caring for and walking a dog sound as time-consuming as taking out the trash. Knowing more about life than I, she wisely said: "You won't regret doing it. But you'll never forgive yourself if you don't."

Connie was one of those women who was able to balance it all—work, children, a husband, and charity work. She skied. She cooked. She knit. She ran a marathon not long before she was diagnosed with cancer. She had even managed to write a book about the history of Coca-Cola based on her experience covering the company for *The Times.* She was tireless.

As she lay dying, she made her husband, John, buy me a book: *The Art of Raising a Puppy,* by the Monks of New Skete, a group of monks who live in a monastery in upstate New York where they breed German shepherds. From the quiet of their lives, they have created an all-consuming method of training puppies that is best characterized as firm and loving with no yelling. It is not unlike books on parenting.

I read the book cover to cover in one sitting. It left me less interested in raising a puppy than in going to live the monastic life in the mountains where time stretched eternally and patience was an instinct. The lessons in the book seemed unreachable for me. The whole process seemed to require reservoirs of time and patience, two things in very short supply in my life. Even the chapter on city dogs didn't seem to consider the frenetic pace of city life. Our life was anything but placid. There must be other books.

Sometime in late October, with just a few weeks of radiation treatments to go, I called Lisa Cannarozzo, a breeder of toy poodles in Florida and the same breeder from whom the Simons had gotten Rocket. Serendipity played its hand. "I only have one little red boy right now," Lisa said. As it turned out, he was Rocket's half brother. It was meant to be. Rich would have to accept that we were going to have a little red dog, not a black one.

"He's so affectionate," she said. "He was born on July 5, so he's still very much a puppy, and he's just wonderful." My own birthday is July 6.

Lisa sounded more like a proud parent than a breeder trying to sell me a dog. "He's so smart, he can already hold it in all night," she said. Then came the sell: "We thought he'd be one of our show dogs, but his ears are too big, which just makes him cuter, really. I'm not sure, though; I promised him to a family in Chicago. If you think you really want him, tell me right away and I'll see about the other family."

Lisa didn't know that she didn't have to sell me on his good looks. Being a show dog was of no interest to me one way or the other. For all I cared, he could have had no ears. It was the part about being so affectionate that mattered to me. I just wanted to be sure Michael was getting a dog who would love him back. By the time Lisa and I got off the phone, the Chicago family had been put off. "I'm not sure they were all that serious," Lisa said. "You can have him."

Kismet. It was meant to be. The conversation with Lisa had a fated quality to it. This was our dog. This was the dog of our fantasies, the dog who had gotten my son through the scare of seeing me go through cancer treatments. I couldn't wait to meet him.

From the time we told Michael he was getting a dog, he had been considering all sorts of names, discussing his list with his friends. He considered naming our dog Chip, after Chip Cody, the surgeon who had removed the cancerous tumor from me. He thought about "Spunky Overboard," the delighted words of unknown origin he squealed when as a very little boy he sent Matchbox cars careening down a four-foot plastic mountain. "Gacky," another possibility, was Michael's imaginary friend who lived in the Central Park carousel when Michael was three. There was Zeus (the suggestion of Michael's friend Jack), Kayak, Cisco, Skippy, Guacamole, and Tuck.

But once we saw our puppy on the Calisa Poodles' website, Michael had no doubt that the sweet, doe-eyed, adorable, seemingly mischievous, auburn-colored puppy was "Huck," a seeker of adventure, like Mark Twain's immortal character. The whole family was in love.

In preparation for Huck's arrival, which was to be

over the Thanksgiving weekend, just days after my last radiation treatment, Lisa and I spoke endlessly. I soon realized that she and her husband, Joe, were themselves in love with our soon-to-be Huck and were having a tough time letting go of him. Lisa kept referring to him as her "love bug," and I began feeling bad about taking him away.

I kept picturing Lisa and Joe in their home in Florida, surrounded by little red poodles, talking to them the way some people speak to toddlers. "Now let Daddy alone." I started wondering what it was like to actually breed dogs. I think I had read too many of Michael's picture books when he was a little boy. I assumed the dogs lived in a barnlike structure and Lisa and Joe lived in a house. Lisa straightened me out. "Oh no, we're all here as one big happy family in the same house," she said. "That little love bug watches TV with Joe every night."

I sent Lisa a check; she sent me a long list of dog paraphernalia to buy in advance of Huck's arrival— shampoo, dog nail clippers, chicken and rice puppy food, ear cleaner, doggie toothbrush, Pepto-Bismol, nutra-cal tube food, and a water bottle. At the bottom of the list of instructions, in capital letters and underlined in red marker, was the message:

ALWAYS HOLD FIRMLY! NEVER ALLOW
OFF LEASH IN AN UNFENCED AREA!

Lisa and Joe were caring, devoted breeders. I felt lucky we had found our way to them. It was only after all of the arrangements had been made that I learned of the world of rescue dogs from a friend. We probably would have adopted a dog instead of buying one from a breeder if I had realized it sooner. But still, I was confident fate had brought us to Huck.

We counted down the months, the weeks, and finally the days until Huck's arrival. A couple of weeks before he was to join our family, on a bright day in early November, Rich, Michael, and I went out to visit Auntie Babs and her family in Ramsey, New Jersey. On our way, we stopped at The Dog Boutique in nearby Allendale to buy everything on Lisa's list and then some. Michael picked out a bed for Huck, toys, several brightly colored leashes, bowls, and a sweater for the cold. He found a mat to put underneath the bowls that said "I love my dog." His face aglow, his smile from ear to ear, his dimples seemingly more pronounced than usual, he showed me the mat and said: "Isn't this just perfect, Mom?" Michael was elated. So were Rich and I.

I I I

The day after Thanksgiving, Lisa put Huck in a crate and onto a plane bound for Newark airport. We had mailed her one of Michael's socks to put in the crate, so he could get used to Michael's scent, and to be a comfort on the plane ride.

Huck was scheduled to arrive at Continental's Terminal C in the QUIKPAK office. Lisa warned us to resist temptation and not open the crate until we were safely home, lest Huck bolt from the crate and out of the airport. "They're like little jackrabbits," she laughed. "You gotta watch 'em."

Flight 1410 left Sarasota at 11:05 in the morning. We left our apartment even earlier. Under normal circumstances, it is about an hour's drive to Newark airport, but we were worried about the crush of Thanksgiving travelers.

To our surprise, there was little traffic, and we were at the QUIKPAK office with hours to spare. For Michael, all of the longing of his young life, the craving to hold and to hug his own dog, was about to be satisfied by a five-pound puppy with big ears and a disposition nearly as sweet as his own. We paced. We squirmed in the stiff, plastic, unforgiving seats in the terminal, just outside the office. We tried to think of games to play to speed the wait. We played Geography and then I'm Going on a Picnic.

I started. "I'm going on a picnic and I am bringing chocolate chip cookies."

Then Michael picked it up. "I'm going on a picnic

and I am bringing chocolate chip cookies for us and a dog treat for Huck."

Then Rich. "I am going on a picnic and I am bringing chocolate chip cookies, a dog treat for Huck, and watermelon."

Back to me. "I am going on a picnic and I am bringing chocolate chip cookies and watermelon and um, uh, um . . ."

"A treat for Huck, Mom. You forgot Huck," Michael admonished.

I don't know if it was the excitement or the chemotherapy fog, but I was already losing I'm Going on a Picnic, and there wasn't much in the basket.

Suddenly, seemingly out of nowhere, there was a lot of activity in the QUIKPAK area. Rich turned to Michael and said, "Mikey, I think Huck is here."

The three of us dashed into the small office. There, on the floor, was a red crate, plastered with stickers that said LIVE ANIMAL. And a handwritten one:

PLEASE DO NOT OPEN. I AM QUICK.

Michael fell to his knees, looked inside and started talking to Huck through the wire door. "Hello, Huckie," Michael said softly.

Michael looked up at Rich and me with a smile as he said, "He's so cute."

I tried not to cry.

Rich said: "He's yours, son."

Michael turned back to the little dog inside the crate, pushing his fingers through the wire opening. Huck began licking Michael's small fingers. "Good boy, Huck. Hello, Huckie. Good boy."

A man in a blue uniform stepped forward and told me I had to sign some papers before we could leave. I managed to do so, despite the tears welling in my eyes. After I signed the papers, Rich picked up the crate. "Let's take Huck home," he said to Michael.

"I love him already," Michael said, as he hugged me very tightly.

"I do, too, honey. I do, too," I said.

And with that, our new family of four headed for the parking lot.

In the backseat of the car, Michael, with the crate next to him, talked to Huck all the way home. "Huck, wait 'til you see where you are going to live. You can sleep in my room."

It was as though Michael had finally found the old friend he had been searching for all his life. He kept sticking his finger through the wire door, trying to get Huck, by now dehydrated and hungry, to take some food.

There was a lot more traffic going toward New York than there had been in the morning going the other way. We were stuck in the thick of it, crawling along the New Jersey Turnpike. Trying to follow Lisa's exact instructions, we still had not taken Huck out of the crate. We had not yet been able to hold him, or, for that matter, get a really good look at him. Huck did not make a sound.

We finally pulled into the garage under our apartment building. Rich gingerly lifted the crate from the backseat, carried it upstairs to our apartment, and set it down on the floor in the living room. Michael sat right in front of it. I gave him an old towel to put across his lap.

I opened the door of the crate. Huck, still woozy from his plane ride, took a cautious step out. Michael tenderly picked him up in his arms and held him against himself.

"I love you, Huck," Michael said. "You are such a good boy. You made it through the plane ride. You did it, Huck."

I looked inside the crate and there, in the back of the crate, tied in a knot, was the white sock of Michael's we had sent to Lisa weeks ago. It had to have been tough for this tiny creature, all five pounds of him, to weather the plane ride. He was stuck in the crate, alongside the baggage. It was so cold in the cargo hold of the plane that the airline did not want to take any responsibility for an animal being able to live through the trip. The carrier required the vet in Florida to sign papers saying the dog could survive in subfreezing weather.

In our apartment, when Huck emerged from the crate and into Michael's waiting arms, he was wobbly and smelled as though he had either thrown up on himself, or urinated, or both. Lisa, in an effort to gussy Huck up, had doused him with some kind of perfume and put a red bow on his head.

I knew the first order of business was to get rid of the bow, get him in the bathtub, and clean him up. At that moment, not everyone in our family found Huck irresistible. In fact, Rich was disappointed. Privately he said to me: "I don't really find him that appealing, but we got him for Michael, not for me, so if he's happy with him, then I'm happy."

Michael tried to get Huck to play a bit, trying to interest him in some of the toys we had bought, but Huck was still shaky, still exhausted from his journey north.

I suggested we give Huck a warm bath. Michael was game and wanted to get in the tub with Huck. We pulled out some of the shampoo Lisa had instructed us to buy. We took the bow out of Huck's now matted hair; Michael put on a pair of shorts and got in the tub. I handed Huck to him, and we carefully soaped Huck up and rinsed him off with the handheld showerhead. Wet, Huck looked so tiny, so vulnerable, and so utterly adorable. I wrapped him in a towel. Michael stepped out of the tub and immediately took Huck into his arms.

Just then the phone rang. It was our neighbor, a member of Rocket's family, Emily Simon, and her cousin, Caroline Bronston. They could not wait any longer to meet Huck. They wanted to come right over. Michael was only too happy to show Huck off. Minutes later, they were at our front door.

The girls squealed with delight. "He's so cute," they said in unison. The three kids sat on the floor with Huck, petting him, taking turns holding him, and trying to get him to chase a ball or eat a dog biscuit. But Huck was so exhausted, he was not responding all that much. He seemed more like a very old dog than a young puppy.

That first night, we did exactly what Lisa had told us to do. We put Huck and one of his new toys in his crate, attached a water bottle to the crate, and said, "Good night, Huck." We had set it all up in Michael's room. Rich and I hugged and kissed Michael, said good night to him, too, and closed the bedroom door behind us. I wasn't sure what would happen next. I assumed that in no time, Huck would start barking or whining.

Ten minutes after Rich and I left Michael's room and collapsed on our bed, Michael appeared at our door. "I don't think I can sleep with Huck in my room," he said. "He makes too much noise when he drinks from his water bottle."

I suppose Michael was so used to having his own room and having utter quiet when he went to bed that the presence of another being, let alone one who was slurping water, would take some getting used to. I thought that feeling would pass in a few days as Huck and Michael became inseparable. It did.

But that first night, we put Huck's crate in the kitchen and turned on a radio. He was perfectly quiet until about three o'clock in the morning when he started barking. As I am sure has been so for every other mother who suddenly finds herself with a puppy, being roused from sleep that way felt an awful lot like the 3:00 A.M. feeding of my child's infancy.

I managed to find my slippers and robe and I stumbled into the kitchen. I felt so sorry for Huck in his crate, barking. Lisa had instructed us to tap on the top of the crate and say, "Quiet, quiet," and then walk away. *But what if he needs to go?* I thought. I followed Lisa's instructions, left Huck in the crate, and went back to bed.

Just as my head hit the pillow, Huck barked again. I put on my slippers again, left the bathrobe behind, and, with Lisa's voice in my ear, went back into the kitchen, tapped the top of the crate and said, "Quiet, quiet, quiet," and went back to bed, this time unable to sleep. I was waiting for the next round of barking.

It took another hour and Huck barked again. This time barefooted, I stumbled into the kitchen and opened the door of the crate. Huck came out and relieved himself on the paper we had put down on the floor. He turned around and walked back into his crate.

Tired as I was, I had to laugh. "Huck, Lisa was right, you are smart. I ought to listen to you," I said. As I turned down the kitchen light, I realized I had already started doing what so many animal lovers do with their pets. I was talking to Huck as though he were a person with complete comprehension of what I was saying. As time wore on, the talking got much worse. I was only surprised that Huck didn't talk back.

The next day, Huck seemed fully recovered from the plane ride and fully adjusted to his new surroundings. His personality started to emerge. He was lively and engaging and incredibly cute. He was always ready for fun. All of the new dog toys got a pretty good workout. Huck was cuddly and quite generous with face licks. He was an unusual combination of sweet and naughty. He wasn't the least bit aggressive and was an insatiable affection hound. He'd instantly roll over on his back for just about anyone who looked like they'd stand there and rub his belly.

On that day, Rich's heart began to melt. Huck stood and watched him shave. When Rich sat on a rocking chair in the living room, Huck went over and put his head on Rich's lap, waiting for Rich's affectionate touch. It took no time before Rich was calling him "Huckie boy" and roaring with laughter when Huck gave Rich's face a bath of licks. A day earlier Rich was dubious about Huck's appeal. Now he was smitten.

Rich had fallen hard for Huck and Huck for Rich. The first time Rich was out of town for an extended period, Huck pulled at a gray T-shirt Rich had left on his desk chair until he was able to get it free. Huck then trotted off with it to his own bed, put it down, and lay on top of it.

I I I

Michael became the envy of friends whose parents had not yet caved in on getting a dog. Jesse, the son of Susan Finkelstein, the woman who kept telling me a dog might be the one thing our kids would have to do without, said he wanted to get the identical dog and name him Tom, so the boys, friends since nursery school, would have dogs named Huck and Tom, a fuller tribute to Mark Twain's vision of boyhood. Another buddy asked his parents for a dog, but the resistance was great, so they started talking about getting a rabbit.

Huck shadowed Michael all over the apartment. When Michael came home from school each day, Huck ecstatically licked his face. While Michael did his homework Huck slept at his feet. When Michael sat and watched TV or played a video game, Huck squeezed into the chair alongside him. When Michael went out-side, Huck waited by the front door.

It was easy to see why Lisa referred to Huck as her "little love bug." He was always looking for someone to stroke his head or his back or rub his belly. He liked to be touched. The moment any of us sat down in a chair, Huck would come dashing over, sit at that person's feet, and rest his head on the sitter's knee, waiting to have his head stroked, waiting to lick a hand.

Huck's unrestrained devotion reminded me of a dog captured in a painting that hangs at the Metropolitan Museum of Art in New York. In *Young Man and Woman in an Inn* by the Dutch painter Frans Hals, a man and woman are reveling at the doorway of an inn. A dog is resting his head in the reveler's hand, content to just be with the man. That was Huck's spirit, too, blissful when he had a lap to sit on or a human hand on which to rest his head.

Huck also loved to play. I had more patience for fetch than either Rich or Michael, something that Huck fig-ured out immediately. One morning, while Rich and Michael were out at Michael's basketball game, I was home with Huck, trying to use the time to get a few housecleaning chores taken care of before they re-turned. Huck was determined to let me know that chores were not really a good idea, that it was really time for the two of us to play ball.

He picked up his favorite orange soft plastic ball and started following me around the apartment until I was still. He dropped the ball at my feet and looked up at me, waiting for me to pick it up and throw it. He'd scamper after it and then bring it back, laying it at my feet again, waiting. After a few back and forths, I tried to bring the game to an end. But Huck was just warming up. He started dropping the ball at my feet, looking up at me, and barking, as if to say, "Come on, let's play some more."

When I didn't respond, he tried other ways to draw me back into the game. I was making our bed when Huck's orange ball came rolling out from underneath it, stopping just at my feet. Huck was lying in wait under the bed until I was close enough, and then, with his nose, sent the ball out to deliver his message. Huck was nothing if not persistent. He fit right into our family.

Huck was ever a people watcher. He'd stand and watch me load dishes into the dishwasher, hoping for a stray scrap of just about anything. He'd stand and watch Michael pack books into his school backpack; he'd watch Rich put his shoes in the closet.

When Huck came to live with us, he was only four months old, full of all the unbridled mischief of a puppy. He'd chase the vacuum, and take all the socks out of the laundry basket, spreading them around the living room floor. He loved to disrupt. Michael would sit down to play the piano, and Huck would wander underneath it, walking in and out and between Michael's legs, making it impossible for Michael to play on. Huck was confused by television and barked at the set whenever a dog was on. He had come to love cream cheese, more than any other treat. All we had to do was say "cream cheese," and Huck would come running.

We were all pretty eager to take Huck for a walk, but there was still a hurdle. Lisa had said we'd need clearance from the vet before we could take Huck outdoors.

The Simons had been our guide on all things involving Huck. There was no question we'd take their advice on vets, too. We took Huck in a taxicab to see Jon Miller, a neighborhood veterinarian with a fun and quirky manner.

"Well, well, whose dog is he?" Dr. Miller asked, as Michael gingerly put Huck up on the examining table.

"He's mine!" Michael said proudly.

After looking in Huck's ears and eyes, taking his temperature, listening to his heart, manipulating his limbs, examining every part of Huck, and then showing Michael how to clean Huck's eyes, Dr. Miller pronounced Huck "perfect." He said we could take Huck for a walk the following morning. And then he added: "I like the name."

We were now ready to take Huck out onto city streets. Our first adventure would be to the Seventy-ninth Street and East End Avenue bus stop, where Michael boarded the city bus for school.

Michael bounded out of bed early that day, eager to walk with his new puppy. We left at about 7:30. I put the collar around Huck's tiny neck and Michael attached the leash. Novices that we were, Rich and I each inspected and reinspected the collar to make sure the fit was right.

Michael, Huck, and I headed out the door, into the elevator, past the doormen, who had already begun to refer to our new dog as "the incredible Huck" (a comical reference to the superhero the Incredible Hulk, capable of feats of superhuman strength), and out the front door of our apartment building. We had barely made it outside when several people, hurrying to work and school, stopped to admire Huck. He had such a sweet face, was so small, and was such an unusual color for a dog that it was hard not to take notice. And then there was the smiling blond boy at the other end of the leash. Together, they looked like an urban Norman Rockwell painting.

Michael held the leash, and we started walking toward the bus stop. Like a toddler who had just learned to walk, Huck wanted to stop and examine every piece of paper, every person, every other dog, every parked car, and every mailbox. The five-minute walk from our building to the bus was starting to look like it would take an hour. Michael, unable to really get Huck to keep walking, turned the leash over to me. My luck wasn't much better. I realized this was not the moment to teach Huck to walk on city streets. Michael was about to be late for school. I picked Huck up and carried him to the bus stop.

Michael stepped onto the bus and then turned to wave at Huck and me, blowing kisses until the bus pulled away. I turned and put Huck down for the walk up East End Avenue and back home. On the walk home Huck was just as determined to explore everything and everyone on the street as he had been on the walk to the bus stop. He'd linger at a fire hydrant and then try to dart across an intersection. I began to wish I were one of those monks.

At one point, Huck started pulling hard on his end of the leash. Before I realized what was happening, he had slipped his collar. I was panic-stricken. "HUCK! HUCK!" I screamed. "Oh no! Oh my God!"

Huck went tearing up East End Avenue. He'd stop for a split second to sniff at something and then take off again. He was a five-pound puppy, loose, with no collar, and no experience on busy city streets. He didn't really even know his name.

I was terrified. I was afraid he'd be hit by a car. How could this be happening? People tried to help, but that just made Huck run more. So did my running after him.

For a moment he stopped to sniff another dog. I was too far away to catch him, but close enough that if I threw my body to the ground, I might be able to fall on top of him. Forgetting all the warnings from my doctors about not getting hurt or cut, that is exactly what I did. I hurled my body on top of Huck.

I now had Huck in my arms. Several people stopped to help. Someone put Huck's collar back on him. I carried him home. Once we were safely inside, I discovered my own bloodied knees and realized that in the chaos, I had lost the scarf I had been wearing to cover my still bald head. It was a metaphor of sorts; our little dog, our Huck, had from the very beginning made all of us forget about cancer and its debilitating emotional and physical effects.

I knew in that moment how much I already loved Huck, something I had never thought about before we got him. I had only thought about how happy he would make Michael. From the moment he arrived, Huck brought a lot of love into all our lives.

Like all new dog owners, it took a while, but eventually Huck and we developed our own rhythms. Michael taught Huck how to high-five. "Give me five, Huck," he'd say as he raised an open hand. Huck would raise a paw and touch it to Michael's hand. "Good boy," Michael would say, smiling triumphantly.

It, too, was a metaphor of sorts. We had closed the

door on a very dark chapter in our lives. We had a victory of our own, and Huck had been our mascot.

I found I had learned from Connie and the monks enough about the fine art of crating, which made training easy enough. Huck never chewed on the furniture or did anything destructive. He had a couple of accidents on the living room rug, but nothing to speak of. After that first day on the street when Huck had slipped his collar, we hired a private dog trainer for one or two sessions, hoping to be taught how to get Huck to walk next to us instead of in front or behind. But it seemed overdone for such a small dog. It was such an over-the-top, New York thing to do. In fact, it was embarrassing. The trainer talked to us about signing a long-term contract, which pretty much put an end to that.

ı ı ı

In early December, a close friend, the same friend who had given me the antique-looking earrings, convinced me to give up my reticence and allow myself to be in the spotlight for a night. She and her husband generously hosted a dinner party to celebrate the end of my cancer treatments.

Michael stood up in front of a room filled with my friends and colleagues and said, "I am really proud of the way my mother has powered her way through breast cancer."

When I looked around the room and thought about how much each of the people there had done for me and my family, I was so choked up, I could not speak. I had had a lot of help getting through it all. The truth of the matter is, I was the one who had cancer, but everyone in that room, along with many people who were not there, had gotten me through it. It was their deep affection and care and compassion that had powered me through. It was Rich's undaunted spirit and Michael's bravery.

The holidays quickly approached. I was especially thankful that year for our many blessings and looking forward to the joy of the season more than usual. Since Rich, Michael, and I celebrate both Christmas and Hanukkah, all December long it feels as though we are either celebrating or planning to celebrate. Our most cherished tradition is cutting down our own Christmas tree. When Michael was about six, Rich located a Christmas tree farm, because he knew it was one of the happiest memories of my childhood.

Ever since then, every December we bundle up and drive an hour and a half to the four-hundred-acre working Jones Family Farm in Shelton, Connecticut, which has been in the Jones Family since the mid-1800s. There are two hundred acres of Christmas trees of all types—Fraser fir, Angel white pine, Douglas fir, Scotch pine, balsam fir, and blue spruce.

Once there, we park the car, pick up a saw from a

basket filled with saws, and climb a path up the mountainside, the snow and ice crunching beneath our boots, in search of the perfect tree. My find always comes early on, sometimes halfway up the mountain, but Michael and Rich always insist the best trees are at the top. So we trudge on.

The Jones Family Farm is a happy place. During one of our hunts, a young man with a bottle of champagne in one hand and a freshly chopped tree in the other came out from the thicket of trees and asked if we'd take a picture of his girlfriend and him. Moments earlier, he had asked her to marry him and she had said, "Yes."

With a brand-new puppy at home, I thought we'd forgo the tree cutting. But tradition being what it is, we didn't. We left Huck at home, drove through the snow to the farm, climbed the mountain, and debated which of several trees Huck would like. Michael, who by then was doing more and more of the sawing, made the first cut and started sawing. He kept at it until his hands were so cold inside his gloves he could barely move his fingers. He turned the saw over to Rich who finished the job.

Once the tree was felled, we carried it down the mountain to a spot where the farm hands took it, put it through a baler (a conelike device that encased it in twine), and strapped it to the top of our car. We then joined the other people crazy enough to do this and

drank hot cider and ate cranberry chocolate chip cookies around an outdoor fire. It was Christmas the way I
remembered it.

When we got home, we carried the tree through
the front door and set it in the stand. Huck didn't quite
know what to make of it and started barking at it. He
soon stopped and settled himself underneath it, where
he stayed while we adorned it with lights and orna-
ments.

We hung four stockings that year, one for Rich, one
for Michael, one for me, and one for Huck. Huck's
stocking had been a gift from the Finkelsteins. It was
red and green and had Huck's name embroidered
across the top. Down the side was the word *woof* and
three paw prints.

On Christmas Eve, before he went to bed, Michael
stuffed Huck's stocking full of gifts he had bought and
carefully wrapped for him. There was no mention of
the gifts Michael might receive; he was completely focused on Huck. "Do you think Huck will really like his
presents?" Michael asked me as I was kissing him good
night.

The next morning, Michael, ignoring the presents
spilling out from under the tree for him, went right for
Huck's stocking. He sat on the floor, pulled Huck onto
his lap, and tried to get Huck to take one of the presents in his teeth to tear the paper. With some assistance

from Michael, Huck ripped the paper off the first present. "Huck, it's a new toy!" Michael exclaimed. "It's a Santa." Huck took the soft plastic squeaky Santa in his teeth, ran around the room, dropped it, and sat right down on Michael's lap again, seemingly waiting for the next present. It was hard to believe this was Huck's first Christmas. He behaved like an old hand.

It went on that way until all the new doggie toys had been opened. It wasn't until Huck's stocking had been emptied that Michael turned to open his own gifts.

And I opened the gift Rich and Michael gave me, a pair of earrings with three interlocking rings to celebrate the strength our small family had shown these past months.

CHAPTER 4

THE POSTHOLIDAY WINTER was long and cold. By March, when Michael had his midyear school break, I was ready for some sun. It was time to hold Auntie Babs to her word, time for her to make up the spare doggie bed. It would be our first vacation since my cancer treatments had ended and the first time we left Huck for more than a few hours.

Michael, a baseball worshipper and die-hard Yankees fan, wanted to go to Yankees spring training. The Yankees were going to play their archrivals, the Boston Red Sox. Rich and I agreed to take Michael to see the Yankees in Florida and decided to add a side trip afterward to a beach resort. Sun, baseball, the beach—the kind of vacation to make me feel young, healthy, and very much alive. No demands, no newspaper, no computers, no phone calls. Perfect.

I had gone through the rigors of cancer treatments fixated on getting myself in shape. The doctors had said that one of the little-understood consequences of the treatments for breast cancer was weight gain. Weight gain? I had always thought chemotherapy leaves everyone depleted and thin. Apparently chemotherapy for breast cancer is different. The depleted part was the same, but the thin part was not. I was determined not to gain weight. Bald AND fat? That really seemed cruel.

All through my treatments, I had spent a lot of hours in the gym doing whatever I had strength for, and I was disciplined about what I ate. I walked everywhere I could. It worked. Despite the months of poison dripped into my body, and the weeks of having my chest, neck, and arm radiated every day, I had come out of it all in better shape than I had been in before it started, back when we sat sipping cappuccinos in Venice.

At a follow-up visit with my surgeon in January, he commented on how fit I was. I told him that exercising had given me the illusion of control over my body. While I am extremely fond of him, and eternally grateful to him, he said in a detached way, "Well, it is just that, an illusion." I wished he would have just let me take refuge in my denial.

For our trip to Florida, I treated myself to a new bathing suit and a pair of white shorts. I bought gobs of suntan lotion and a new hat, having thrown away the one I had to wear the previous summer to cover my then bald head. In fact, I had thrown away or given away just about everything I owned that was in any way cancer related.

Once I had enough hair to go to work comfortably without a scarf, I took out the stack of scarves given to me by dear friends, washed and ironed each one, wrapped them in tissue paper, and gave them to a woman I knew who was suffering through chemotherapy for the second time. Nearly everything else went into the trash. It was as though I had the garbage collector carry away all the pain and fear that had insidiously become a part of our daily lives. We had a new life now. We had Huck.

The night before we left for Florida, we took Huck, his oversized round pillow of a bed, a turquoise-and-white plastic sneaker that squeaked when he held it in his teeth, his red leash, his red jacket, his food, and a container of cream cheese to the Clarks' house in Ramsey, New Jersey. Huck had been there only once before for a few hours on Christmas Day.

Huck could not get comfortable in the car. Like a lot of New Yorkers, he'd never had a real reason to be in a car, and the trip to New Jersey was one of only a handful of rides he had ever had. I held him on my lap, and he settled a bit, but trembled for most of the forty-five-minute car ride across the Hudson River and up through the foothills of the Ramapo Mountains in northern New Jersey.

I felt a little like trembling, too. I was glad Rich was driving. I still didn't feel entirely competent behind the wheel of a car, one of the stranger and unexpected side effects of the cancer treatments. Although my hair had now grown enough to look short chic rather than bizarre, other parts of me were returning more slowly.

At some point over the last eleven months, I had lost my ability to intuit. I found that I could not rely on my gut instincts, whether it was about what Michael wanted for dinner or which angle of a news story to bear down on. It was unnerving. I had an unfamiliar skittishness about my own judgment.

I mentioned it to my doctor, who thought it might be part of the intellectual fog that can be a side effect of chemotherapy. But I always felt it was something deeper. It was as though I had lost depth perception about life. I felt uncertain a lot of the time. I was unable to judge just how far I would fall if I made a wrong decision.

It eventually wore off, but on that cold March night, terra firma seemed hard to find. As we drove through the darkness, I started wondering if it was a mistake to leave Huck in a place so unfamiliar to him. The Clarks had a busy life of their own. Barbara commuted into Manhattan every day. Dave worked. Darian, the only one of their three children young enough to still live at home, played on assorted sports teams. Maybe I was taking advantage of their generosity. I suddenly felt more of a sense of melancholy than excitement. I shook it off.

We drove down Ramsey's Main Street, past the stone-faced Episcopal Church with the red doors, past Veterans Park with its monument honoring World War II veterans, past the stately looking high school, over the train tracks, past the bank, the hardware store, the ice cream shop, the movie theater, and the library; past all of the symbols of the small town's pride and fierce sense of community.

There are six churches in Ramsey. Volunteers run the fire department, and the sports teams, as well as dozens of civic organizations. The town's leaders haven't allowed a Gap or a McDonald's to replace the mom-and-pop shops.

In its earliest day, residents of Ramsey grew strawberries by the railroad-cars-full and sent them to New York. The town has pre–Revolutionary War roots and takes great pride in the oldest house, which dates from that period. For much of the 1900s, there was a sign in town: RAMSEY—ALTITUDE 410 FEET—THE 3RD HEALTHIEST PLACE IN THE UNITED STATES. Makes me wonder what the first two were.

Every fall, just when the leaves begin to turn bright yellow and orange and the air is crisp, the town holds

"Ramsey Day," complete with a parade, fire engines, flanks of Girl Scouts and Boy Scouts, at least one marching band, and generations of Ramsey residents who turn out to celebrate their life there.

People like Fred Swallow, whom I once met at Ramsey Day, show up. A tall, kind-looking man, a retired barber and World War II veteran, Fred mans the VFW booth, selling white T-shirts for the post with a picture of a giant bald eagle flanked on either side by American flags and the words TAKING PRIDE IN THE UNITED STATES OF AMERICA.

Fred had gone to barber school in New York after serving in the army as a lab technician; he was stationed in New Guinea and then the Philippines, where he worked to protect soldiers from the ravages of malaria and syphilis.

One of his army buddies came from Wayne, New Jersey, and in 1948 enticed Fred to seek work in Ramsey. Fred eventually bought the barbershop in the Ramsey train station, called it Fred's Barbershop, and stayed there for thirty-three years, raising the price of a haircut over that time from 90 cents to $7.00. It was a life he loved.

For Fred, the protected world of a barbershop in the Ramsey train station was threatened not by the advent of unisex hair salons but by the Beatles. "We had four chairs. Everything was going good till the Beatles came," he said, looking back on his entrepreneurial days in town. "After that, the kids stopped coming for haircuts."

But pastoral Ramsey is also the kind of place where teenagers grow restless. Even as the town celebrates its community, the police are on hand to talk to teenagers about the lethal combination of drinking and driving.

Ramsey is nestled between the township of Mahwah and the borough of Allendale. The clusters of houses are separated by dense woods, hills, and small lakes. The stillness of the suburbs is a welcome respite in the warm weather months, but feels weighty, empty, and desolate in the winter. In those months, the streets are deserted, the yards vacant. Church on Sunday is as much a social gathering as a prayerful one.

On that cold night in mid-March, Ramsey was at once welcoming and bleak. I had no particular relationship to the town other than that it was the place where my sister and her family had lived for more than a decade. Small-town life had a certain dreamy appeal to me, but I had become too ironclad a New Yorker to ever make that kind of life my own.

We pulled into the Clarks' driveway and parked under the bare trees and the basketball hoop. Their house is on a busy street and is set back from the road by a deep lawn and a split-rail fence. There is a detached garage, with wood stacked on either side, and a big backyard, fenced in for their dogs.

I stepped out of the car with Huck's leash tightly

wound around my hand. I put Huck down on the ground, and he immediately started to explore. The air was bracing, filled with the comforting scent of fireplaces. The black night sky was a patchwork of stars.

Rich, Michael, Huck, and I walked up the stone path, past the garden with the stone that says "Dad's Garden," to the front door. Not surprisingly, it wasn't locked. We walked in with Huck and all his paraphernalia. The television was on, the fire in the fireplace crackled. Barbara and Darian were curled up on the couch, under the vaulted ceiling in the living room, watching television. They were each wearing black sweatpants and tight-fitting blue shirts, which set off their blond hair. They looked more like sisters than mother and daughter.

Darian, a year younger than Michael, was thrilled to see Michael and to have Huck as a houseguest. The cousins immediately whisked Huck up the stairs to Darian's room, where all three of them lay on the floor. Although she had not yet spent much time with Huck, Darian already loved him, in part because of her closeness to Michael. She had a talent for drawing, and on the Thanksgiving Day before Huck arrived at Newark Airport, she had sat making welcome signs for our new dog.

"You're sure you brought enough stuff?" Dave quipped before taking the bags from my arms and giving me a kiss on the cheek. "How much does he weigh again?"

As we walked into the kitchen, Dave started explaining to Rich that he had filled in the holes under the fence dug by one of their dogs, lest Huck slip under it. Rich had been worried about the holes. Dave had also moved a boulder in front of a place in the fence where he thought there was too much distance between the bottom of the fence and the ground.

Listening to Rich and Dave talk about the fence, I couldn't tell if Dave was accommodating our usual overwrought level of concern about things, or if he, too, was worried about Huck slipping underneath the fence. Life at my sister Barbara's house was always more relaxed than at mine. It wasn't just the country mouse–city mouse divide. Barbara and Dave never would have bought a second Corky as we did to protect against the loss of Michael's most cherished childhood stuffed animal. They would have had a lot more confidence that Corky would not be forgotten in the backseat of a car or, if he was, that they'd be able to get him back, or if they couldn't, that was okay, too.

Admittedly Rich and I watched everything in Michael's life too closely, more likely an affliction of parents with one child than parents with three children. The difference in our parenting styles allowed Barbara and Dave a lot of laughs at our expense. When the kids were very young and we'd come for a visit, Barbara and Dave were content to have Michael and Darian play outside in the yard without parental supervision.

I wasn't. I spent all my time at the window watching the kids play. Maybe I had lived in New York too long, where venturing outside without an adult is a real rite of passage. Or maybe it was because Darian was the youngest of three children and Barbara and Dave had let go of all of their instincts to overprotect. No matter, they loved to poke fun at me.

Michael was often the beneficiary of his aunt and uncle's more adventurous approach. One winter afternoon, when Michael was a toddler and Rich was away, Michael and I went to visit the Clarks. There was a lot of snow on the ground and Dave suggested we all go tubing down a nearby hill. I considered myself something of an expert sledder, having grown up in Connecticut, but tubing was new to me. There is no way to steer a tube. A wooden Flexible Flyer can be steered away from a tree. As far as I could tell, a tube leaves the rider no way to avoid calamity other than to bail out of the tube. Needless to say, I wasn't a fan.

Dave said he'd take Michael down the hill. I was reluctant. But Dave quietly nudged me and, to Michael's unending delight, Dave won out. With Michael in his lap, Dave rode the tube down the ice-slicked hill. As soon as they reached the bottom, Michael jumped out of Dave's lap and shouted with delight, "Again!"

From the time Michael was born, Barbara had made an effort to have her own close relationship with Michael, and he loved her for it. It was no surprise that when my cancer was first diagnosed, Barbara called Michael and told him that if he ever needed someone to talk to, he should call her.

Darian and Michael had a special kind of closeness, too. When they were young and the heat of summer made the tar in the streets of New York melt underfoot, we'd get in the car and go to the Clarks. Darian and Michael would sit in a wading pool together, pouring water over each other's head, and eat Popsicles, their faces covered with the frozen treat's bright colors. It was such a simple pleasure, but an indelible marker in Michael's childhood. They'd dig in the garden looking for worms, they'd chase each other around the yard, and then they'd get back in the pool.

When they got too big for the wading pool, they'd trade turns swinging on a tire Dave hung from a tree in the yard. They'd stay outside until it was dark enough to chase fireflies. On more than one occasion, Michael ran to me and said: "Mommy, I'm having so much fun. Can we come back tomorrow?" His skin moist with perspiration, his face tanned from the sun, his dimples popping, his blue eyes sparkling, he smelled of the outdoors. I'd draw him close, hoping to still the passage of time, but in a matter of seconds he was off again.

As the kids got older, baseball and a devotion to the Yankees took over. There were treks to nearby Finch

Park to practice throwing a baseball and catching it in a glove, and sliding in the dirt. Back at the house, they'd play Wiffleball in the yard, giving both Rich and Dave a chance to reawaken their own ball-playing muscles.

That night, as we stood in the kitchen and I unpacked Huck's belongings, I told the Clarks about Huck's habits. "He goes out three times a day, but he is also paper-trained, so if you can't take him for a walk, just put down some paper."

"We don't need the papers, we'll just let him out in the yard," Dave said. "You worry too much."

I told him about the cream cheese. "It's his favorite treat. Whenever you want to reward him, or even if you just want to call him, just say 'cream cheese,' and he'll come running."

Dave and Rich chatted about baseball and the games we were going to see in Florida. I paced around nervously. Barbara teased, "Would you relax? I think we know how to take care of dogs," she said, pointing to the multiple beds of their multiple dogs. "He'll be fine."

I admired my sister. I had felt very protective toward her all through our years of growing up. By virtue of being the youngest, not to mention the third girl, she had gotten the brunt of all the problems of our childhood. But Barbara really didn't need protecting; she was scrappy as could be.

Barbara had been a high school cheerleader with a

penchant for drama, two characteristics that draw people to her even as an adult. She was always the energy in the room.

As an adult, she has a powerful sense of family, loyalty, and order. She is also a "clean freak," like me, something I am sure came out of the tumult of our youth. It conveys a sense of order even when none exists.

Dave is a quiet man who is often hard to read. He's given to small acts of kindness and always deflects attention from himself. Other than Barbara's commute into New York for work, the Clarks rarely venture into the city.

Barbara and Dave are a perfect match. His reticence complements her high wattage. Dave has a runner's build and a narrow range of expression. His own parents died young. Every summer he packs up his family and takes them to the races at Saratoga, something he did as a child. Dave loves to garden, play baseball, and run. He prides himself on knowing his way around a kitchen, a skill he picked up at Cornell's School of Hotel Management. He and Barbara were married at Cornell, and they return every year to hike the rugged hills of Ithaca and to eat the meatball sandwiches sold off the back of a truck dubbed "The Hot Truck," something Dave relished when he was in college there.

Dave and Barbara are passionate about Ramsey, the town where they have raised their children. They have each coached various Ramsey girls' softball teams. Dave went so far as to volunteer his time to serve as commissioner of the league, which included nine towns. After about a decade of service, Barbara and Dave retired their bats and gloves. The town thanked them with plaques and invited them to throw out the first pitch on Opening Day.

Throughout the fall, on Saturday mornings, Barbara goes to the high school to help sell hot dogs and sodas at the game, engaging her fellow Ramseyites in conversations about their lives.

Barbara is the kind of person people want as a neighbor. She can be counted on to notice if you went away and forgot to close the garage door, or to pick up your kids if you were running late, or to make a pan of lasagna if you had a family member in the hospital. I knew she would take good care of Huck.

I left Dave, Barbara, and Rich chatting in the kitchen and started up the stairs to see what Huck and Michael and Darian were doing. As I got closer to the top, I heard barking and laughing. Standing in the doorway of Darian's room, I watched Huck doing what he does best. With one paw planted on one of Darian's cheeks, he was licking her face, her eyes, her nose, and her ears. It was as though he were holding her face with hands. "If he likes you," Michael said laughingly, "he could lick your face for hours."

It was getting late. "We have to leave in about five minutes," I said to Michael.

Michael responded the way he always did when I tried to pry him out of Camp Clark, the house where all the fun was. "Can't we stay?"

I responded the way I always did, "No, we have to get going. Five minutes."

Truth was, I wasn't ready to leave either. I wasn't ready to leave Huck. I wouldn't be any more ready in five minutes or five hours.

I went back downstairs, through the living room, pausing by the piano to look at the latest addition to the family pictures, this one of Michael and Darian at a dance recital of Darian's. The family resemblance strong, they could easily be brother and sister. I carefully put the picture back down on the piano and went into the kitchen.

I said to no one in particular, "We'd better get going."

Barbara put her arm around me. "Now you guys have to have some fun. You deserve this vacation. Have a fantastic time," she said. "And please, do not worry about Huck. He'll be fine!"

We all walked back into the living room. I stood at the bottom of the stairs and called to Michael. He and Darian came down. Looking at Darian holding Huck in her arms, I thought about how even though Huck

had nearly doubled in size since the day we got him—
he now weighed nine pounds—he was still a very small
dog. He was just the perfect size to hold; he seemed so
vulnerable. I wondered if he would miss us as much as
we would miss him.

It was time to go. I braced myself. "Bye, Huckie," I
said. I gave him a pat on his head.

Michael took Huck from Darian and looked him
straight in the eyes. "You be a good boy, Huck," Michael said. "I love you."

Rich, too, was having a hard time. "Okay, Huckie
boy. We'll see you soon," he said.

Rich gave Huck a hug. Michael handed Huck back
to Darian. Barbara walked with us out to the car. "Seriously, Jan, don't worry. Just have a good time," she said.

Rich, Michael, and I got into the car. Rich immediately tried to save the moment, saying ebulliently, "Is
this family ready for a great vacation?" He pulled the
car out of the driveway. We drove back through Ramsey's dark streets and back to the highway. Rich started
filling Michael in on the latest Yankees trivia he had
picked up from Dave.

I had a terrible sense of foreboding. I thought it could
be many things or it could be nothing at all. But it was
there, a dull ache, something I decided to ignore, hoping it would just go away.

When we got home that night, our apartment felt

empty, as though someone was missing, which of course, someone was. Huck had been living with us for only four months, but it was already hard to imagine life without him.

The next morning, as we were about to board the plane, my cell phone rang. "I just wanted to let you know Huck is fine. He's sound asleep in my lap," Barbara said. "We love having him here, especially Darian."

It was reassuring. We got on the plane. Michael and I took out a deck of cards and spent the next few hours playing crazy eights and laughing at the reruns of *Everybody Loves Raymond* they were showing on the plane.

CHAPTER 5

I LOVE THAT MOMENT on vacations when the plane touches down and you realize the bonds of your everyday responsibilities have fallen away. Whatever adventure you have embarked on is yet to unfold, whether across an ocean or across state lines. That is exactly how it was when the plane touched down in Tampa. It was a moment of possibility and excitement.

After being confined in an airplane seat for three hours, with its scant leg and elbow room, I stood up, pulled together the books and magazines I had toted onboard, the giant bottle of water, my needlepoint project—all barely touched. Freedom. It is hard to know whether I felt freed from the captivity of the plane or freed from the demands of daily life or freed from the nightmare that I had been living in for so long, but it didn't matter.

"Welcome to Tampa," the pilot said. "The temperature here is 75 degrees."

As I walked off the plane, I thanked the pilot, the copilot, the flight attendants, just about anybody I could find. Never, ever had I been so happy to be in Florida. I was practically giddy. By the time we got there, I didn't even miss Huck all that much. I was glad to have left the responsibility of walking him three times a day and worrying about him to someone else for a while.

I had been to Florida before—mostly while covering presidential campaigns. I also had been there to visit Rich's mother a few times, and once to visit a family friend, but never on a true vacation. Florida always felt too hot, a state in need of shade trees. Not this time. It was forty degrees warmer that day than it had been in New York. We peeled off our jackets and sweaters and headed for the car rental counter. It was only about 10:30 in the morning, the day was still fresh, and we were ready to take on Tampa.

In its heyday, Tampa was a city of laborers who culled the surrounding waters for phosphates and shrimp. They also once produced a fair amount of the world's hand-rolled cigars.

That was then. Now Tampa's waterfront is full of gleaming steel office buildings and banks and fancy restaurants, with boats tied up outside. It is not nearly as interesting as it must have been in the cigar days. Still, no matter what time of year you might visit, you're bound to find a professional sports team in midseason. They have a baseball team, a hockey team, and a football team. They have a minor-league baseball team. They even have a women's football team called the Tampa Bay Terminators.

There must be something strategic about Tampa's location in the middle of the water with Tampa Bay on one side and the Hillsborough River on the other, both emptying into the Gulf of Mexico. MacDill Air Force Base and Central Command take up about six thousand acres of the city's real estate. Part of that acreage is used to protect endangered species, including the bald eagle. The Persian Gulf War and the campaigns in Afghanistan and Iraq were run from that base. Some of the generals liked it so much, they stayed. Generals Norman Schwarzkopf, who ran the first Gulf War, and Tommy Franks, who ran the second one, both now private citizens, are said to live in the same gated community in Tampa. I'll bet their neighbors feel safe.

We picked up our rental car and headed for the hotel. We were staying at the Hilton Westshore, close to the airport and to the Yankees' winter home, Legends Field. For more than thirty years, the Yankees had played their winter games in the eastern part of the state, in Fort Lauderdale, in a stadium named for the city. But George Steinbrenner, the owner of the Yankees, was from Tampa and spent most of his winters there, so he decided to move the team to Tampa.

George Steinbrenner owns the Radisson Hotel in Tampa and decreed it the team's official hotel. But the million-dollar ballplayers don't stay there. If I had done some decent reporting beforehand, I might have been able to figure out the team's habits—where they ate breakfast, or where they bought gas—and we could have planned to accidentally run into Derek Jeter or Jason Giambi.

Our hotel wasn't downtown near the water, or even out near the wetlands and the bald eagles; it was near the Yankees, near their practice fields, their stadium, their souvenir shops. We stayed out that way for Michael. He wanted to breathe the same air as the team.

There isn't much else for tourists in that part of Tampa, except for several shopping malls, the flashiest of which is the International Plaza. Full of upscale stores, like Nieman Marcus, Tiffany, Louis Vuitton, and Burberry, it is the Madison Avenue of Tampa. Shopping malls are now ubiquitous in just about every corner of the country except Manhattan. For Manhattanites, when all else fails, malls are a tourist attraction.

I had remembered to pack everything for a sun and sand vacation except the most essential item—my sunglasses. I reminded Michael and Rich to pack theirs, but didn't remember my own. Rich suggested a visit to

Neiman Marcus. I suggested we find a drugstore. Rich won.

We walked into the store past the Fendi handbags, and the Jimmy Choo handbags, and the Chanel handbags, all displayed like museum pieces under glass, to the sunglass counter. I actually found a pair I could more or less afford, or maybe I was still intoxicated by the warm air and just talked myself into thinking I could afford them. But I now owned a new pair of Kate Spade sunglasses.

As the saleswoman handed Rich back his credit card, he asked, "Do any of the Yankees shop here?"

"Oh, yes, Derek Jeter buys his jeans here."

The day was only getting better. Maybe Derek Jeter would walk by the sunglass counter on his way to buy jeans. Anything was possible. We decided to get lunch. The saleswoman pointed to the escalator. "You'll find a lot to eat upstairs. There are all kinds of good restaurants up there, anything you want."

As the escalator climbed we found ourselves underneath hundreds of white butterflies made out of some kind of sparkling fabric that were suspended from the ceiling. For a moment, it felt oddly otherworldly. We walked outside, past the Häagen-Dazs shop, and the Nestlé Toll House counter, to the open-air rows of restaurants.

The pathways near the restaurants were designed with Europe in mind. Strolling the painted brick walkways, an active imagination might be reminded of Sienna, Italy. I said the painted stucco walls of some of the eateries reminded me of a kind of faded burnt-orange color we had seen a lot on our trip to Italy. Michael said the color looked more like nacho cheese. It was all about imagination.

We found a small Italian restaurant, Pizza Roma, and sat at an outside table. Michael and Rich ordered a three-cheese pizza. I ordered a salad. I could sense how content Rich was in that moment. "It was so balmy. I was so at ease, so relaxed," he would later say. "I thought it was just delightful. I was with my family. Our vacation was all in front of us."

We discussed how excited we all were to see the first of several baseball games that night. For any Yankees fan, it was a matchup to savor—the Yankees versus the Red Sox. They would not meet again until May. Johnny Damon, a former Red Sox player, now a Yankee, would be facing his old team for the first time. Best of all, we were going to the game with our close friends Mimi and John Kepner, whom we had met on a Nantucket beach years ago.

John and Mimi, college sweethearts, married young. When I first saw them playing Wiffleball in the sand, it was hard to discern that they were the parents. They looked so youthful I thought they and their sons were part of the same group of teenagers. John, in his early fifties, was so agile, a hitter and runner, and every bit as strong as his teenaged boys, Tim and Dave. Mimi, with her baseball cap and dead-on pitches, seemed no different from Tim's and Dave's teenaged girlfriends, who were also playing. If anything, Mimi seemed more game. Before I knew her name, I thought she had set an impossible standard for motherhood.

Our affinity with the Kepners was instantaneous and strong. No sooner had we met than we found ourselves spending every day of our vacation together, lolling on favorite beaches, and trading barbecuing nights. Every summer afterward, we and the Kepners tried to schedule our Nantucket vacations for the same weeks.

The friendship quickly moved beyond Nantucket. We'd visit the Kepners at their house in Pennsylvania over Christmas and they'd come to see us in the city in the spring.

Our families shared many passions—baseball, Nantucket, biographies of historical figures, biking, Wiffleball, watching the sunset over the water, board games, and standing around on Main Street in Nantucket at night listening to Tim and Dave play the music they usually performed with their entire band, called Full Service.

The Kepners felt like family. Tim and Dave treated Michael like a younger brother. Tim, who had played semipro baseball, spent endless hours throwing a baseball with Michael on the beach. Dave let Michael tag along just about everywhere he went. When Michael was very young, John taught him how to throw a football and to play the Kepner family baseball game invented by John, "dice baseball."

The Kepners were Philadelphia Phillies fans first and Red Sox fans second. John would torment Rich and Michael by wearing his Red Sox cap to the beach every day.

By sheer coincidence, Tyler Kepner, the oldest of the Kepner sons, is a sports writer who covers the Yankees for *The New York Times*. He would be covering the Yankees game against the Red Sox that night.

After we finished our lunch that first day in Florida, we went back to the hotel for a swim before the game. I sat on a chaise lounge with the sun on my face and felt completely healthy for the first time in a long time.

We met John and Mimi for an early dinner. Michael wasn't much interested in dessert. He wanted to get to the ballpark early to watch the teams warm up. He was hoping to catch a stray ball, or get a player's autograph, things that were nearly impossible during the regular season. Proximity to the players is what spring training is all about.

On the way into the stadium, we passed a table full of Yankees paraphernalia. Michael, a child who rarely asks for things, spied an unusual Yankees cap that must have been left over from St. Patrick's Day. It was green, with a shamrock on the right side of the bill. Michael stopped his mad rush into the stadium long enough to look at the hat. "Now, that is a lucky hat," he said to me. He picked it up and ran his fingers over the shamrock before putting it back on the table.

"Do you want me to buy it for you?"

"Let's get it tomorrow. I don't want to miss getting balls and autographs."

We headed for our seats. They were in the sky. Section 217, Row P, Seats 1–5. We were closer to the yellow foul pole than we were to home plate. You could see the faces of the players, but could not make out their expressions. "I'm going down to the fence," Michael said, as he took the concrete steps, two by two, and headed toward the field.

The stadium was starting to fill. Some of the trappings were a lot different from those at Yankee Stadium in the Bronx. For one thing, some people were walking around eating giant turkey legs. The only other place I had ever seen people do that was in Disney World.

But other things about Legends Field were the same as Yankee Stadium. The outfield fences were the same dimensions. And the raucous, passionate fans were no different in Tampa than they were in the Bronx, like the freckled-face boy wearing a T-shirt with a giant baseball on it and the words GET TOUGH OR GO HOME. It was a T-shirt with attitude.

At Legends Field, just like at Yankee Stadium, there were constant reminders of the Yankees organization's unbridled chase for money, even if it meant quashing the spirit of young fans. Two hours before the start of the game, old men in khaki pants and yellow shirts with the word USHER on the back stood guarding the field-level seats, keeping anyone without a ticket for one of those seats from getting a close-up look at the players. I don't know how Michael slipped through, except that he must have learned something from his mother, the journalist, about getting into places unnoticed.

He stood patiently up against the fence, waiting and hoping. No balls or players came his way, until finally, one of the Red Sox did. It was Terry Francona, the team's manager. In his excitement, Michael had forgotten to take a program with him for signatures. He took off his Yankees World Series cap and handed it and the pen from his pocket to the Red Sox manager. "Wrong hat, kid," the manager said with a smile. He signed it and gave it back to Michael.

It wasn't the signature of one of Michael's beloved Yankees, but it was nonetheless a signature of one of baseball's greats. John Kepner would be impressed.

We settled into our seats under a setting sun, the sky streaked with orange and red. The temperature started to drop. The groundskeepers wet down the dirt, chalked the batters' boxes, the catcher's box, and the foul lines. Everyone in the stadium stood and sang "The Star-Spangled Banner," always one of my favorite moments at any game, and the first pitch was thrown. More than ten thousand New York and Boston fans were now packed into the stadium for the show-down.

Michael sat between Rich and John, whose encyclo-pedic knowledge of the game of baseball matched Michael's. Michael never took his eyes off the game, and he never stopped talking.

Johnny Damon was booed by many in the crowd the minute he walked onto the field. Other players were hit by pitches. One of the Red Sox plunked one of the Yan-kees in the back. The emotional intensity of the game was so high it felt more like a game in the World Se-ries than an exhibition game in the Grapefruit League. Bernie Williams hit a home run for the Yankees in the second inning. Rich and Michael jumped up and started pumping their fists in the air and high-fiving each other.

By the middle of the game, I was getting cold, and despite the intensity of the matchup, I was starting to get bored. Mimi and I set off to see if we could find some-thing to warm us up—hoping for hot tea, hot chocolate, or depending on our level of desperation, sweatshirts.

We walked past the stand where the turkey legs were sold, past the stand that sold smoked crabs (another delicacy not sold in Yankee Stadium), to the hot dog counter. There was no tea, no warm drinks, just beer, lemonade, water, and soda. We passed it all up and went into a small souvenir shop, mostly for a chance to warm up. We decided to forgo the overpriced sweatshirts. We made our way through the aisles of pencils and snow globes and shirts and hats, bumper stickers and balls, and went back outside again.

We were not far from the vendor selling the green hats with shamrocks on the bills. I went over and looked at the green hats one more time. There were only two left. I decided to buy one for Michael. I knew he wanted it, but had been too excited to stop long enough to buy it on our way in. Who knew if it would still be there on our way out of the stadium that night. I bought it and stuffed it into my purse.

By the time we got back to our seats, Mimi and I had spent so much time walking around that we weren't that cold anymore. Tyler had wandered down from the press box and filled Michael in on how Jorge Posada had been taken to the hospital before the game after taking his eye off a pitch that landed somewhere between his left eye and his nose. Michael loved the baseball gossip and the camaraderie.

For me, the greatest pleasure of the night was watching Michael. I was so happy to see him so happy.

The game had been tight all along, but the Yankees pulled ahead in the seventh inning, 5 to 3. Things tightened again in the eighth inning, but the game ended just perfectly, a 5–4 Yankees victory. We walked out of the stadium in high spirits singing "New York, New

York" along with the recording by Frank Sinatra that is pumped in after every Yankees game.

I handed the hat to Michael. "I hope this brings you a lot of good luck."

"Oh thanks, Mom. I love it. I can't wait to show it to Jack."

Michael's buddy Jack loved the Yankees, too, and had a fondness for St. Patrick's Day. I was reminded of another spring break when we had come to Florida to visit Rich's mother. Michael was only about five years old, and scatological humor could still produce a belly laugh. After seeing a sign that said "Butt's Road," he was desperate to call Jack to laugh with him about it. The boys were too old now to find Butt's Road very funny, but they would both like a green Yankees baseball cap with a shamrock on it. I was sorry I had not thought to buy one of the caps for Jack. I saw the vendor on our way out of the stadium and asked if he had any green hats with shamrocks left. They were all gone.

"Will you have more tomorrow?"

"No, that's it for this year. All our lucky greens have been sold. You'll have to wait 'til next Paddy's Day." I was glad I had already secured a lucky hat for Michael.

Back at the hotel, we sat and had a late-night snack with John and Mimi, and then said good-bye to them. They were heading home in the morning.

We then went to our room. Michael, basking in the

glow of a Yankees victory over the Red Sox, was already planning the next day's events. He wanted to go to the Yankees practice fields near the stadium to watch the minor leaguers during their morning practice. He also wanted to go swimming in the hotel pool. We had a lot on our to-do list before tomorrow night's game against the Texas Rangers.

We were all exhausted. Michael could barely keep his eyes open long enough to change his clothes and brush his teeth. He got into bed and then out again, pulling a picture of Huck out of a book in his backpack and standing it up against the lamp on the bedside table next to his new green Yankees cap and his baseball glove. "Good night, Huck," he said. He fell asleep as soon as his head hit the pillow.

I was already feeling the effects of having some distance, physical and emotional distance, from New York. I was starting to relax, something I had not done in a long time. The interruption of routine, so dreaded after my cancer diagnosis, was now a welcome respite. But as I got into bed and realized neither Rich nor I had to take Huck for his nighttime walk, I thought about Huck, staying in what to him was a strange house. I asked Rich if he thought Huck was okay. "I'm sure he is, but you can call Barbara tomorrow if you want to put your mind at ease."

CHAPTER 6

THE NEXT MORNING, we set out under an overcast sky to find the minor-league practice fields. The concierge at our hotel directed us to a park where old-fashioned, simple, green stands separated two baseball diamonds. So depending on which way you sat, you could watch the action on either of two fields at the same time. By chance, there was a minor-league scrimmage in progress on each of the diamonds. We sat there for a while watching some young players hit the ball a distance that surprised even them, while others missed routine plays. Michael and Rich critiqued the players.

All this baseball led Michael to start thinking about his own upcoming seventh-grade baseball season. He wanted to take advantage of the warm Florida weather and get in some practice. Rich, who had brought his glove to Florida under the assumption that he'd be pressed into nonstop catches during our time at the beach, suggested we stop at a nearby Sports Authority and buy a glove for me, too. That way Michael would have a pitcher and a fielder for his practice.

I knew there was a method to Rich's madness. Throwing a baseball around on a field in Florida was a long way from having chemotherapy dripped into my veins. It was a good idea, physically, spiritually—just a good idea.

So off we went. Back on the road, we stopped at the Sports Authority on Kennedy Boulevard where I tried on dozens of gloves. I had no idea what one looks for in a glove, so I took Rich's and Michael's word for it when they urged me to take the soft, tan outfielder's glove made by Wilson. I had never owned a baseball glove. When I was growing up, girls didn't play on school base-ball teams. While we walked to the register I put the glove on my hand, punching my fist into it to make it mine. I imagined myself becoming every bit as good a baseball mother–player as Mimi Kepner.

We headed back to the hotel to change and swim in the pool. I had wanted Michael to have some lunch be-fore we went swimming, but he insisted on swimming first, saying he was still full from the pancakes he had eaten for breakfast.

We were the only people at the pool. The sky was growing dark. Still, Michael was the first one in the water. With an eye on Michael in the pool, Rich and I sat down for a moment, talking about the plans for the beach part of our trip. "Come on, Dad," Michael called. "Come on. I've got the football."

"Give me a minute."

Just as Rich stood up to take off his T-shirt and dive into the pool, it started to drizzle. The sky was getting darker by the minute. I was the killjoy. "Come on, Michael, it's starting to rain. You have to get out of the pool."

"Let's wait and see if it stops," he called.

"It is not going to. Come on, let's get some lunch. If it stops, we can come back later."

A dripping, disappointed, suddenly hungry Michael got out of the pool, wrapped a towel around himself, and asked: "What are we going to have for lunch?"

We went upstairs to change. Rich stretched out on the bed. Michael grabbed the remote control, turned on the TV, and started surfing the channels looking for *SportsCenter*. I was about to go into the bathroom to take a shower when my cell phone rang.

"I'll bet it's *The Times*," Michael said. "If it is the paper, don't answer it," he went on. "You promised you would not do any work."

"I have to answer it." I grabbed my phone and looked at the caller ID. It wasn't the paper. It was Barbara. "It's Auntie Babs."

I flipped open the phone. "Hi."

"Jan, I'm at work. I conferenced Dave in. He's on, too."

"What's wrong?" I didn't want to hear the answer.

Our room was suddenly silent. Michael had turned the television off. I could feel him and Rich staring at me.

In a cracking, barely audible voice, Dave said: "Janet, I am really sorry, Huck ran away this morning. We've looked for him all day. He's gone."

I couldn't speak. The shock and pain nearly overwhelmed me. I looked at Michael while I was trying to absorb Dave's words. I could not bear it. I handed the phone to Rich.

"Dave."

Dave repeated to Rich what he had just said to me. Huck was gone.

"Oh, no. Oh, no."

At just that moment, Michael put the pieces of the conversation together and threw himself at me, sobbing uncontrollably. "WHAT HAPPENED TO HUCK? IS IT HUCK?"

Before I could answer, he yelled again, "JUST TELL ME. WHAT HAPPENED TO HUCK?"

I tried not to cry. "He ran away."

Michael was screaming and crying. The cries were visceral, as though he were in excruciating physical pain. I held him. His whole body was shaking. His cries were so loud, Rich could not hear Dave.

Rich raised his voice. "When did this happen?"

In a very slow, quiet way, Dave began to step Rich through the morning's events. He recounted the story that is every dog owner's nightmare, the nightmare that makes it so risky to give your heart over to a pet in the first place. For our family, our little Huck represented nothing less than the affirmation of life.

"It was about seven thirty. I went out to the driveway to get the paper like I always do."

Barbara kept interrupting Dave. "Has Huck had a rabies shot?"

"We'll get to that, honey," Dave said to Barbara.

Then he continued. "I came through the backyard and locked the gate behind me. Huck was out in the backyard doing his business. I was standing in the drive-way looking around for the paper and the next thing I knew Huck was barking and running down the drive-way. At first I called to him, but he wouldn't come. Huck would just not come to me. I kept trying to catch him, but every time I reached for him, he ran from me."

Barbara started to talk over Dave. "Has Huck had his rabies shot?" she asked again.

Impatiently, Rich turned to me. "Janet, has Huck had his rabies shot?"

"Yes, yes, why?"

Rich tried to continue with Dave. Rich was doing

his best to keep his own emotions at bay, concentrating fully on getting the facts. He was now speaking in forceful tones. "Barbara, he's had his rabies shot. Now, Dave, this happened when?"

"It was early this morning, before Darian went to school. In fact, she didn't go to school today; she stayed home to help look for Huck. She's really upset."

Rich could not piece the story together fast enough. "Dave, how did Huck get out?"

"He is so small and so skinny, he must have been able to slip through the part of the fence where it meets the gate," Dave continued. "There are about three inches there. I don't know if he saw me on the driveway getting the paper and wanted to follow me, or if he just wanted to get out of the backyard. I just don't know. But all of a sudden, there he was barking, running around between the front yard and the driveway. Whenever anyone came near him, he'd run. Darian tried to get him to come to her. And if he'd go to anyone, he'd go to her, but he wouldn't. At one point I was able to grab hold of him from the rear, but he turned and sank his teeth into me, which surprised me. It wasn't a very good place on his body to grab him, but I didn't have a choice. And then once he started biting, I couldn't hold on. Barb was trying to leave for work—she was all dressed and was in heels—but she came running out of the house to try and catch him, too."

Barbara was still worried about what Huck had

done to Dave. "You should see my husband's hand. He can't use it. I want him to have a doctor look at it. He won't go."

Rich, whose sharp mind always functions with laser-like precision, kept trying to bring the conversation back to the time line. "I'm really sorry about your hand, Dave. Let's come back to that in a minute. Finish telling me what happened."

Dave's voice had now grown a lot steadier. "It was the morning rush hour, there was a lot of traffic in front of the house. There is some construction going on about a half mile up Wyckoff Avenue, so everything was kind of backed up. At one point, Huck was at the end of the driveway and I was worried he would dash out into the road and get hit by a car. Barb went out in the street and stopped the traffic. Darian and I kept try-ing to catch Huck. People in their cars were watching what was going on. Huck just kept running between the front yard and the driveway. People walking to school stopped to watch. A lot of horns were blaring because of the traffic mess. At one point a heavyset guy driving a truck stopped, got out of his truck, and started walk-ing toward Huck, and making all these noises at him. I guess the guy thought he could make Huck run back toward the house. But that didn't happen. The guy just scared Huck even more. Huck tore up Wyckoff Avenue, in the direction of Hubbard School. I was still in my robe and slippers and Darian was still in her pajamas, but we all went running after him, including Barb in her high heels. We kept calling him, but he just kept going. I can run pretty fast, but he outran us right away. Darian ran up past Oak Street, but she lost him, too. At that point Barbara had to get to work. Darian and I have been out looking for Huck all day. She wouldn't go to school."

Rich was finally getting the picture. "What about your hand, Dave?"

"He got me pretty good. Like I said, I was really surprised he would do that to me. But it's all right. Barbara thinks it's worse than it really is. There was a lot of blood, but I don't think there is any real damage. It is kind of swollen right now. I'll be okay."

"I'm very sorry Huck bit you like that."

"Rich, we're the ones who are sorry. I don't know what to say. I feel terrible. We are all so upset. "

"We're upset, too," Rich said. "Let us figure out what we're going to do and I'll call you back. What kinds of things have you been doing to find him?"

"I called a friend of mine who lives up that way and he said he saw Huck run by. This guy said he didn't think Huck would run past where they're doing the road work. So we've been driving around looking for him in all those streets back there. But we haven't seen him. I called some of the police stations and veterinarians within a five-mile radius. Darian has been working on a sign. I can expand the radius if you want me to."

"Yes, of course, do that. It couldn't hurt," Rich said.

Rich now wanted to get off the phone with Barbara and Dave so he could collect his thoughts. "Let me call you back in a few minutes when we know what we're going to do."

Meanwhile, Michael had not been able to stop sobbing. I tried to both hold him and reach for Rich's cell phone at the same time. Working the phones was intuitive for me. I wanted to start calling the airlines to find out how soon we could get on a plane. There was no question in my mind that we were going to go home and look for Huck.

"You shouldn't come home," Barbara said to Rich. "We can put up a sign and keep looking for Huck. You should stay and try to enjoy the rest of your vacation."

"I don't know what we're going to do," Rich said. "Let me talk to Janet; I think she is on the phone with the airlines. I'll call you back."

Rich hung up the phone and reached for Michael. But Michael pulled away and reached for his suitcase, still only half unpacked, and started throwing his clothes into it. In soft tones Rich started to explain to Michael what had happened.

"When Uncle Dave went out to get the paper off their driveway this morning, Huck somehow got through the backyard fence. Uncle Dave tried to catch him and so did Auntie Babs and Darian, but they couldn't. Huck ran up Wyckoff Avenue. Uncle Dave and Darian have been looking for Huck all day, but they have not been able to find him."

"Is he dead?" Michael asked.

"A friend of Uncle Dave's who lives in the direction Huck ran in saw Huck, but I don't know when that was."

It was now about 3:30 in the afternoon. We'd soon be facing rush hour. I was having a hard time convincing American Airlines to find tickets so that we could fly home right away. I begged the woman on the other end of the phone to find us seats, on any airline, for anytime that afternoon or evening. She said there was nothing for the rest of the day. I begged some more. I told her we had to get home for a family emergency and then explained to her what the emergency was. I was grateful to be put on hold. I thought it was a good sign.

I told Rich he ought to start packing, too. He paused, then said, "Is this the right decision?" and then didn't even wait for an answer. "Tell her we have to get home, tell her to let you speak to a supervisor, ask if we can just come to the airport and be on standby."

While I waited on hold, I looked over at Michael. Our son's heart was shattered. Our little eight-month-old, nine-pound puppy whom we had left in a strange place was now lost. Forget the ball games. Forget diving into the Atlantic Ocean and lying on the beach with a book. Forget feeling carefree. Forget trying out that new baseball glove. Nothing mattered now but finding Huck.

"Ms. Elder?"

"Yes, yes."

"I can give you the last three seats on our last flight out of Tampa. It leaves at 6:02."

"That's great. We'll take them. Let's just exchange the tickets we have for next week out of Palm Beach for the tickets out of Tampa tonight."

"I'm sorry, ma'am, I can't do that."

I don't remember what she said after that until she came to the part about the tickets costing $500 a piece—one way from Florida to New York, $500 times three—$1,500, just to get us home. Buying more tickets also meant we were now stuck with three return tickets out of Palm Beach. The woman's assurance that we could save the Palm Beach tickets and use them anytime in the next year was cold comfort.

I knew we didn't have a choice. I gave her my credit card number, took down the flight number and our reservation numbers, and got off the phone. By the time I did, Michael had stopped crying, his eyes were nearly swollen shut. "I'm packed. Can we go?" he asked.

"Just give Dad and me a few minutes to pull everything together and we're out of here."

I called down to the front desk to ask if they'd get the bill ready. I explained that we'd have to be checking out now instead of tomorrow morning because our dog ran away and we had to get back home to look for him. "Would you hold on for just a minute?" the clerk asked. I started using my free hand to pack. "Ma'am, there will be no charge for tonight. We'll have your bill ready for you in five minutes. Just stop by the desk on your way out. I hope you find your dog."

No gesture ever made me feel more kindly toward a hotel. It eased the $1,500 sticker shock of the plane tickets. "We'd like to give our Yankees tickets away. Can anyone at the desk use three tickets for tonight's Yankees game?"

"That's very nice. I'll ask around."

I hung up and started to pack, hurriedly explaining to Rich that our vacation just cost $1,500 more, although we had been saved some money by the hotel. He was only half listening to me. Rich had turned all of his worry inward and was blaming himself for Huck's disappearance.

"I knew it, I just knew it. That's why I was worried about the holes under the fence. It's my fault. It is no one's fault but mine. I felt it in my bones. I don't know why I went ahead with this arrangement if I thought something bad might happen. I never should have rolled the dice. I should not have put Huck in this position and

I should not have put the Clarks in this position. It is my fault. I am so mad at myself."

Of course it wasn't Rich's fault any more than it was my fault or Barbara's or Dave's. But there was no talking to Rich about it in that moment. I knew he was as heartsick as I was and worried that our rush home would just set Michael up for more anguish. It was another roll of the dice.

I asked Rich to call Dave back and tell him we were on our way. "Ask him if it's really cold. We may have to go by our apartment first to get our winter jackets."

"We have to go home first anyway; we need our car."

"Let's just go," Michael pleaded. "Can't we just go straight to the Clarks? We can use their car."

I didn't want to involve Michael in all of the arrangements. "Just tell Dave we're on a six o'clock flight; we'll be at their house around ten. Oh yeah, and ask him for the name of that hotel we once stayed at near their house, the one we stayed at over Thanksgiving."

I looked at the clock. We didn't have much time to make our flight. We had to get out of the hotel, drive to the airport, return the rental car, get our tickets, and get through security. I stuffed my clothes in my suitcase, along with the new baseball glove, my books, and my needlepoint project. There was no point in putting any of it in my carry-on bag.

My cell phone was losing its charge. I knew there

were countless calls still to make once we got to the airport, so I put the phone charger and my Palm Pilot in my handbag along with a pad and pen. I started rummaging through Michael's suitcase to pull out anything with long sleeves. The air on the plane would be cold. New York would be even colder.

Rich called Dave to let him know our plans and find out about the hotel. "It's the Woodcliff Lake Hilton on Tice Road. You sure you want to come home?" Dave asked.

"We have to, Dave."

"OK. Well, Darian is working on the sign."

"That's great. Tell her to write that there is a reward—$1,000—cash."

Michael was sitting on the floor, with his back up against one of the beds. "Let's make it $2,000," he said to Rich. "I can put in the other $1,000 from all of my birthday money in the bank."

Rich reached out and touched Michael's shoulder. "A thousand dollars is a lot of money," he said to Michael. "It is enough to get people to pay attention. Anyone who would look for Huck for $2,000 would look for Huck for $1,000. We don't have to use your money."

And then Rich was back to Dave: "A thousand-dollar reward, Dave."

"Wow. Okay."

"Oh, and Dave, I think you might have a picture of

Huck. I sent one to Barbara in an e-mail when we first got Huck. You probably still have it, and if you do, Darian could use it on the sign."

"Okay, we'll check. We'll see you later."

Rich was calmer. No doubt he was already working out the game plan. I was busy trying to get us out of Tampa and into a New Jersey hotel. That was the easy part. I knew Rich was wrestling with the impossible—figuring out how we were going to set out to find a tiny dog in an unfamiliar wooded mountainous area. He had already decided on a $1,000 reward. He had already realized that the Clarks had a picture of Huck buried on their hard drive.

"Is everyone ready?" I asked.

"Let's make sure we have everything," Rich cautioned. He started to look around.

"Dad, let's go. It doesn't matter if we left anything."

Michael then put on his green Yankees cap. With each of us toting a suitcase on wheels, the mood somber, we headed for the lobby. The bill was ready. No one was interested in our Yankees tickets.

"Wait," I said to Rich who was rushing ahead. "Michael still hasn't had anything to eat. We have to find him a sandwich or something."

"Mom, no."

"There's nothing in the hotel," Rich said. "We'll find him something at the airport."

Out in the hotel parking lot the wind was starting to pick up. Michael's cap blew off and he chased it down the row of cars. A man who had just parked and stepped out of his car grabbed the hat before it landed in a puddle. He handed it to Michael. "This looks like one you wouldn't want to lose," he said.

Michael responded softly, "Thanks."

CHAPTER 7

WE MUST HAVE radiated panic in our demeanor. Here we were, in the Tampa airport headed back to New York after a vacation that had lasted about thirty hours. The clerks at Hertz, the woman at the airline ticket counter, and just about everyone else we encountered in the airport went out of their way to be helpful. The airport was crowded with travelers, many of them tanned, now headed for colder climates, a fact given away by the wool coats folded and draped over their arms.

We were consumed with worry, surrounded by potted palms and ceiling-to-floor windows that allowed the bright afternoon sun to flood in. At one point, as we looked for the airline counter, we found ourselves standing beneath copper pelicans hung from the ceiling, looking past signs that said things like SUN COUNTRY. It was surreal.

We gave our Yankees tickets to a young man behind the American Airlines counter as we picked up our tickets. "Feels like my lucky day," he said at having strangers hand over three free baseball tickets. "I haven't been to a game at all this year, and I never got there last year because I was unemployed and couldn't afford the tickets. So thanks, thanks a lot. Are you sure I can't give you something for them?"

"No," Rich said. "Just hope for us that it turns out to be our lucky day, too."

We walked to security and stood at the end of the long line, taking off our shoes and putting them into the gray plastic tubs. Rich knew he would be stopped. "Why don't you and Michael go ahead to the gate and I'll catch up to you. See if you can find him something to eat."

"Okay. Do you want me to get something for you to eat?"

"Get me anything."

The titanium prostheses in Rich's hips always set off the metal detectors in airports, making his experience with airport security particularly onerous. The routine never varies. Before he walks though the metal detector, he tells the security guard that he has two artificial hips that will surely set the thing off. But it isn't until after Rich walks through the metal detector and it starts beeping that the security guard calls someone over to investigate Rich further. Rich is then pulled aside while the security people go through his carry-on bag. Then they take a handheld metal-detecting wand and wave it over his entire body. When the wand reaches Rich's hips, it starts beeping loudly, at which point a male security guard pats Rich down. Surely there is an easier way to make sure that someone with an artificial joint or two isn't concealing something illicit.

As we usually do, I went through the detector first and then Michael. Rich was still emptying his pockets.

"You'll have to go back through and take that hat off, young man," the security man said to Michael.

Michael took off his green Yankees cap, put it in a plastic bin, and pushed the bin down the length of the rolling metal tubes until it was pulled along through the x-ray machine. Then he walked back through the metal detector for a second time. I handed Michael his shoes and his hat and said, "Let's go find something to eat."

"Mom, I don't want anything to eat."

"Well, Dad's hungry, so let's go find something for him, and we'll get you something just in case you get hungry on the plane."

"I really don't want anything, and I won't want anything on the plane either."

"Okay. Let's get something for Dad."

We walked through the airport quickly, as though getting the food fast would get us back to New Jersey sooner. Under other circumstances, Michael would have laughed at the sign that read FRANKLY GOURMET and would have wanted to see what an airport gourmet hot dog looked like. But I didn't point it out. We stopped at an utterly nondescript stand with ready-made sandwiches stacked inside one refrigerated metal cooler and bottles of soda, juice, and water lined up in another. There were a few metal baskets with bags of chips and cookies on the counter alongside the register.

I grabbed three turkey sandwiches and three bottles of water, trying to make quick work of it before Michael told me not to buy as much as a bottle of water for him. I paid the uninterested, massively overweight woman sitting half on and half off a wooden stool, taking people's money and handing them back their change with as little verbal interaction as possible.

I was struggling to hold the bag of food and get my change back into my wallet as an impatient Michael started rushing away from me. "Hang on, let me just get my money put away," I called to him.

"I just want to get to New Jersey," Michael said. "There is nothing we can do until we get there. I hate being in this airport."

I managed to slow him down to a walk instead of a run, and we made our way back to the departure gate. It was crowded with children under the age of five and their frazzled-looking parents. One mother was traveling alone with twin infant girls, each dressed in a pink dress with white daisies, each clutching a pink stuffed dog, each crying.

I was distraught. All I could think about was how to help Michael deal with this level of heartbreak. He was in so much pain. I wondered if I had made a mistake in thinking getting a dog would spare Michael the anguish of watching his parents deal with a terrifying disease. Wasn't this agonizing, too?

Rich was already at the gate and had thrown his bags over three of the fake leather seats. He seemed angry. I didn't want to ask him why. I didn't know if the security people had given him an especially hard time, or if he was still blaming himself for Huck's disappearance, or if he had some business call that had upset him.

"I got you a turkey sandwich," I said.

"Thanks. I'm going to walk over to where it is quieter and start making some phone calls. Why don't you and Michael sit here."

"Okay. But I can start making some calls, too."

Rich suggested I call Lisa, the breeder from whom we had gotten Huck. "Maybe she's heard of this happening with some of the other poodles she has raised. Maybe there is something about the breed that we should know or maybe she has some ideas about how to go about finding him. And, oh yeah, ask her if he can really withstand subfreezing temperatures overnight."

Michael dropped his body onto the chair. I put my arm around him.

"Mom, do you think Huck has been hit by a car?"

"No, I don't think so. He's very smart, you know. I really do think he's smart enough to stay out of the street."

"He must be really scared."

"I'm going to call Lisa. Do you want me to walk away to call her or do you want to listen?" I asked.

"I don't care."

I dialed Lisa's number. It was sheer coincidence that the town where Lisa lived, the place Huck had been born, was not all that far from the Tampa airport.

Lisa answered the phone in a jovial voice so incongruous with what I was feeling. I hated having to deliver the news.

"Oh, no, oh, that little love bug," Lisa cried out as I told her we had left Huck with relatives in New Jersey and he had run away. "Why didn't you bring him with you to Florida? You know these little guys are great travelers and lots of hotels let you bring pets."

I suddenly felt completely incompetent. "It never really occurred to us," I said somewhat defensively. "My sister is a very experienced dog owner."

"Oh my, oh no, this is just terrible. I hope no one steals him," Lisa said. "I would say you have to just keep looking and looking. I don't really have any special advice. I'm just really worried someone will pick him up and keep him. I'd maybe call some of the vets there, in case someone brings him in."

"Lisa, how much cold do you think Huck could tolerate? Do you think he could survive in subfreezing temperatures?"

"Well, I don't know. The vet down here said he could survive in some pretty cold temperatures—you know we had to get that all approved before we sent him to you—but I don't really know how much cold he could take and for how long. He's only eight months old; he may not even be full grown yet."

"Do you think he could survive overnight in temperatures below the freezing mark, below 32 degrees?"

"Oh, I just don't know. I'll bet your son is just, oh your poor son, he must be heartbroken. Oh dear, wait 'til I tell Joe. Please, call me and let me know what happens."

I was glad she didn't want to discuss any further why I had thought it was okay to leave Huck in New Jersey.

I turned to tell Michael what Lisa had said and only then realized he had wandered off. I had a moment of panic, but then spotted his green baseball cap down by the next gate. His hands were in his pockets, his head was down. He was slowly shuffling along the blue-and-white tiled floor.

As I watched him make his way back to our seats, I thought about what Lisa had said about someone stealing Huck. Despite my own childhood nightmare of having a dog stolen, it had never occurred to me that someone would steal Huck.

"What did she say?" Michael asked.

"She said we should look and look and look."

"What else did she say?"

"She said we should call all the vets in the area, because someone might take Huck into their own house and then take him to a vet."

"You mean someone might steal Huck?"

"Yes, that is what she was saying."

"I'd rather someone steal Huck and take good care of him than have him be killed by a car."

I was still trying to absorb Michael's ability to put Huck's well-being above his own emotions when he said: "Mom, if we don't find Huck, I don't ever want another dog."

"We can talk more about that, but I understand."

By now Rich had been gone for a while. There was movement around the boarding gate. People were starting to line up to get on the plane. I started to wonder just where Rich had gone to make phone calls and who he was calling.

"Where's Dad?"

"I don't know, honey. He should be back any minute."

Michael and I stood; I picked up the bag with the sandwiches and the water and started to walk toward the gate.

"Mom, seriously, where is Dad?"

"I don't know."

The waiting area was now nearly empty. Most of the passengers were either on the plane or on the line to get on the plane.

I was about to call Rich on his cell phone when he appeared. "I'm sorry I took so long. Did they call our row yet?"

"We were one of the first ones called. We must be toward the back of the plane."

"I'm sorry. I just had to clear my head. I had to try and figure out how we get a quick education on what people do when things like this happen. I called Miller's office."

It took me a few seconds to remember that Miller was Dr. Miller, the vet.

"Did he have any good ideas?"

"He wasn't there, one of his office assistants was there. She said dogs usually go where the traffic is. She thought it was possible he is running along Route 17."

"I just don't believe that," I said. I didn't want to believe it. Route 17 was a highway.

"I know. I don't really believe that either. She lost me when she said Huck might be headed for the George Washington Bridge. That just sounds totally implausible. She did have one good suggestion. She said we should make sure the reward sign says 'heartbroken boy.' She said people would be more likely to respond if they thought there was a child involved. I do think that's a good idea."

Then he paused and whispered out of earshot of Michael: "But, you know, if she is right about Huck running toward the traffic and running toward Route 17, there is no telling how far away he could be by the time we get to New Jersey. It also dramatically increases the likelihood of him being hit by a car."

With that horrific thought in our heads, we fought our way down the tight aisles of the plane toward the back. We did indeed get the last three seats on the plane. They were in the last row, right up against the bathrooms. Because there was not a row of seats behind our row, it felt even more confining, more claustrophobic than plane seats usually feel. Michael sat by the window, I sat in the middle, and Rich sat on the aisle.

We fastened our seat belts and tried to settle into our seats. Michael looked at both Rich and me and said: "Whatever happens, we can't let the Clarks feel bad about this." He then leaned forward, put his elbows on his knees and his head in his hands, and began to sob. I rubbed his back. There wasn't much else to do or to say. Michael had always turned to me to soothe him. This was the first time I could remember when nothing I could do or say would console him.

Rich turned to me and quietly said, "You know I needed this vacation, we both needed this vacation, but I have to switch modes now. Michael is going to be looking to me for a certain attitude, for strength. I don't have the luxury of feeling anything else. I can't feel bad about Huck being lost right now, because that is a distraction and a waste of the time I need to think and to look for him. I have to be tough. I don't know where this is going. We are in uncharted waters. I have no idea what this is going to take."

It was as though Rich just needed to hear himself say it all out loud. It was as though he were talking to himself. He didn't wait for me to respond.

"I can get in another call before the plane takes off," he said while reaching in his pocket for his cell phone. "I'm going to call the Finkelsteins."

"Why them?" I asked.

"They always have good ideas. Susan just might know someone or something. Besides, she and Rick love us and will understand how important this is to us."

Susan Finkelstein is always at the other end of her cell phone. I do mean always. Her friends tease her for her constant state of hypervigilance, but they are the same people who count on it as well. I am sure she is listed as the person to call in case of an emergency on dozens of school forms.

In my very early days at *The New York Times*, I once covered an event where Barbara Walters was being given an award. She was introduced by Roone Arledge, who, at the time, was president of ABC News. Commenting on Barbara Walters's relentlessness and resourcefulness, he said if he were stranded in a foreign country, or taken hostage anywhere in the world and he could make only one phone call, he would call Barbara Walters. I would call Susan Finkelstein.

"This is all wrong. This should not be happening to you," Susan said when Rich told her why we were now on a plane heading back to New York. "This is just wrong."

Rich had reached the Finkelsteins in California where they were spending spring break.

"Susan, I need you to think about this and help us figure out what we should do to find Huck."

"We will. Let me just get Jesse. He's been having an all-day tantrum about going to Disney instead of this really cool museum. I'm sure he'll want to talk to Michael."

Just then, the flight attendant announced that we were about to depart and all cell phones would have to be turned off.

"Listen, I'm going to have to shut off my phone. I'll call you when we land. Talk about it with Rick and Jesse and Sophie. See if you have any ideas."

"Okay, okay, we will. Have a safe flight. Call us when you get in."

The Finkelsteins had been touring the very off-beat Museum of Jurassic Technology in Los Angeles when Rich called. Susan hung up with Rich and turned to her husband, Rick, and said, "They're doing this really

crazy thing. Huck ran away in New Jersey and they're
going there to try and find him. It is crazy. You know
this is the first vacation they have had since the cancer.
This is just crazy."

Rick agreed. "That dog is gone. It's over."

Meanwhile, we were filled with more of a sense of
hopefulness, or at least purpose, as the plane banked
skyward. There was a certain relief in finally being air-
borne. At least we were getting physically closer to New
Jersey, however incrementally. For a minute or two, Michael also seemed relieved. I suggested he take a bite of
his sandwich. By now it was after six o'clock at night.
Michael had not eaten since nine o'clock that morning.

He reluctantly agreed. I handed him the triangular
box the sandwich was in and opened one of the bottles
of water and held it in my hand. He picked up the rather
stale-looking turkey sandwich with both hands, stared
at it for a moment or two, and then bit into it. He looked
out the window and then back at me.

"Can you take this away? I feel sick."

I took the sandwich off his lap and handed it and the
water to Rich.

"Mom, I think I'm going to throw up."

Michael reached for the bag in the back pocket of
the seat ahead of him, leaned over, opened up the bag,
and threw up into it. After a minute or two that seemed
more like an hour, he sat up, his face full of perspiration,

and handed me the bag. I handed the bag to Rich. Rich was about to stand up to go and dispose of the bag when Michael said: "I still feel sick, don't take the bag away."

For the rest of the three-hour flight from Tampa to New York, Michael was either throwing up or resting his head on my lap. The physical space we were occupying felt like it was getting smaller. The odor from the bathrooms right behind our seats grew more offensive as the flight wore on. The woman with the twin infants was pacing up and down the aisle with one baby in each arm.

Rich sat with his eyes closed. He thought fleetingly of his own childhood and the dog he had grown up with, Flash. Flash was a sweet-faced little rogue, taking off from time to time and getting into fights with other dogs before wandering home, battle scarred. Rich's memory was that his mother braced herself for the worst by announcing each time that Flash was probably not coming back, that he was lying dead somewhere on the side of the road. This, in turn, always frightened Rich. Sitting on the plane, trying to think through the details of finding his own son's runaway dog, he thought of Flash and of himself as a boy, and how wrenching it was to worry about the life and death of a cherished dog.

I thought back all those years to Michael's tender loving care of Inchie, the worm. This was much harder. After he had pined so much for a dog, after he had gone through the confusion and fear of watching his mother being treated for cancer, after he had fallen head over heels in love with Huck, I was worried that if anything happened to Huck, the hole in Michael's heart would be scarring.

There would be a hole in my heart and Rich's heart, too. I leaned my head against the back of the seat and closed my eyes and all I could see was Huck's small face and big brown eyes.

I thought of the way he stands on his hind legs, with his front paws on Rich's and my bed, whenever we are lying there reading. He just stands there, staring up at us, waiting for someone to stroke his head. Toy poodles are especially adept at standing on two legs instead of four, which makes them all the more likely to be treated like people. Huck is a master at standing straight up on his hind legs—at the kitchen counter, the side of the bed, the couch, the piano bench, and the front door.

I thought of the way Huck sleeps—in his own little blue bed, curled up in a ball, with his head reaching around to his tail and his legs tucked underneath him.

About halfway through the flight, when night had fallen, and the sky was dark, and the lights on the plane low, Michael looked at me and asked, "Mom, what should I do?" I thought he was talking about what he should do to make himself feel better physically. But he wasn't. He was asking a deeper question. It was a plea for some psychic relief from the emotional trauma.

"I keep thinking that Huck might have already been hit by a car. And when I'm not thinking that, I have this image of him all wet and cold, trying to find something, lying under a bench, nosing around a garbage can and you can see in his face how scared he is, you see in his eyes how helpless and lonely he is."

"All we can do right now is to try our best to focus on all of the instincts Huck has for survival," I said. "And we can try and think of as many good ideas as we can about how we might find him. Sometimes it helps if you think of what you would advise someone else to do."

It was the best motherly advice I could come up with at the moment. But the truth was, I was scared, too. The thought of Huck cold and alone was utterly wrenching. The thought of Huck lying dead by the side of a road was unbearable.

Something occurred to me that had not occurred to Michael, and I was uncertain whether or not it had crossed Rich's mind. Huck could have been attacked by another animal. He ran away in a heavily wooded area, full of wild animals like bears and coyotes and raccoons and birds of prey. Huck was raised to live with people. I don't think he had any instincts for fight. I couldn't imagine him trying to fight off the attack of another animal.

"Ladies and gentlemen, please turn off any electronic equipment; return your trays and seat backs to the upright position. We are beginning our descent into New York. The temperature there is 42 degrees."

I was fixated on that 42 degrees. I wondered how many degrees colder it was in northern New Jersey than it was at LaGuardia airport. If the temperature did not drop much lower, and if Huck were still alive, I thought he'd be able to make it through the night without freezing to death.

Our seats in the back of the plane meant we'd be the last people off. Michael said he felt light-headed, which was no surprise given how much he had thrown up on the plane. I was worried about him. He was by now so completely drained, part of me just wanted to take him home to his own bed.

Mercifully, we did not have to wait long for our bags. While we waited Rich called Mimi and John Kepner to tell them we were no longer in Florida and never went to the Yankees game. "Mimi, if you have any ideas of how to handle this, let me know."

"I will. We'll call you tomorrow regardless. Good luck."

Rich also called Susan back. Jesse asked to talk to Michael.

"I'm really sorry about Huck," Jesse said. "I told my mom you should try and get on the radio and tell people to look for him."

"Thanks, Jesse." Michael then handed the phone back to Rich.

Susan said the family had talked it over and come up with a few ideas—an ad in the newspaper, a call to the ASPCA, and Jesse's suggestion for the ad on the radio. They were all good ideas.

We picked up our bags and headed as fast as we could out of the airport, into the cold night air, and into a taxi. From the cab I called the garage where we keep our car and told them to expect us in twenty minutes and to please have the car ready. Riding across the Triborough Bridge, I felt as though we had only been away from New York for an afternoon.

When the taxi pulled up in front of our building, Rich and Michael went directly to the garage to get our car and I went upstairs to grab our winter parkas. When I put the key in the door, I half expected to hear Huck on the other side. I walked into the dark apartment and opened the walk-in closet in the entryway in search of the jackets. I had enough presence of mind to also grab a couple of flashlights. I stepped backward, out of the closet and onto one of Huck's squeaky balls, the orange one we usually used for our game of fetch. I stopped and stared at it for a moment, tears welling in my eyes before I turned and rushed out of the apartment. I ran through the lobby and, as I did, Ed, one of the building's doormen, asked if everything was all right. "I thought you were on vacation."

"We were, but Huck ran away, so we came home to find him."

"Oh no, where was he staying?"

"With my sister, in New Jersey."

"I hope everything works out. That's really too bad. I hope you find him."

"I hope so, too."

CHAPTER 8

R ICH AND MICHAEL sat waiting in the car in front of our apartment building. I opened the car door and tossed the jackets and the flashlights onto the backseat next to Michael, who looked like he was asleep.

Outside, the New York City air was cold and damp. There was no hint of spring, just more of winter's bite. It was the kind of March night that makes you want to draw the curtains and batten down, to crawl into bed early with a good book, a far cry from what we were setting out to do.

"The flashlights were a good idea," Rich said.

"I was hoping we could spend some time tonight actually looking for Huck," I said. "Maybe that is completely crazy, but I don't think I can live with myself if we don't drive around a bit and at least try."

"Does that mean we don't have to stop at the Clarks'

house?" Michael asked, with his eyes still closed. "Can we start looking for Huck as soon as we get there?"

"I think we have to stop at Auntie Babs's house so Uncle Dave can show us exactly the area where he thinks Huck ran to," I said.

"Can't we just call Uncle Dave?" Michael asked earnestly.

"I think we have to go to the Clarks' house and see what kind of progress they've made," I said. "We won't stay there for long, but let's make their house our first stop."

Although my instinct was to start walking up and down the dark streets calling to Huck the minute we got there, I knew it made no sense. Rich agreed and Michael did, too, reminding us of what he had said earlier. "We have to make sure the Clarks' don't feel badly about this."

"We all agree on that score, angelpie," I said. "None of this is anyone's fault."

I knew Rich wanted to jump in and blame himself again, but he didn't. Instead, he met Michael's eyes in the rearview mirror and said: "Michael, I promise you, we're going to do everything we possibly can to find Huck. We'll do whatever it takes."

Michael did not respond. His eyes were now open. He sat perfectly still on the backseat.

We drove north on the FDR Drive and over the

George Washington Bridge and into New Jersey. For most of the ride through the darkness, we didn't say much to each other. It had been only a few days since we made the same trip to New Jersey to take Huck to the Clarks, our vacation stretching in front of us.

Now, with our vacation abruptly and sadly ended, instead of feeling restored, we were emotionally and physically depleted, about to begin a desperate search through the deep and barren backwoods, empty lots, ponds, streams, and mountainous terrain of northern New Jersey, a search that more than likely would prove futile. I looked at the blue neon numbers on the dashboard: 10:30. Huck had been missing for fifteen hours.

I called Barbara to tell her we were on our way.

"Darian made a sign, and she and Dave have already put some up," Barbara said. Her voice started to quiver. "You know I can't tell you how bad we all feel."

I did not want her to cry. Hearing my younger sister cry over the phone would only have made me cry. I was too weary not to be pulled into it. "Michael is the first one to say that none of this is your fault," I said. And then trying to get her off the phone, I added: "We'll be there soon and we can talk. We've just crossed the bridge and are on Route 4. We'll be there in about half an hour."

I looked out the window. We passed one shopping mall after another, each closing for the night, with only a few cars parked under the floodlights in the vast lots. I turned to look at Rich who was sitting stiffly at the wheel, concentrating on the road ahead.

I pulled down the visor so I could look at Michael in the mirror on the back of it. He was fingering the brim of his green Yankees cap and looking out the window. At times, he'd press his head against the window, as though he had seen something or someone, and then he'd pull back again.

I thought about how tired we all were and realized I had never made arrangements for us to sleep anywhere that night. "I'll call that hotel," I said to Rich. "What did Dave say the name was?"

"It was a Hilton. It was the Woodcliff Lake Hilton," he said.

"I'll get their number. How many nights should I tell them we will be spending there?"

"Tell them we don't know."

The hotel clerk was polite and took the reservation quickly. He asked for a credit card number. I could not remember mine but didn't need to. Rich's number and the security code were part of the readily accessible catalog in his head.

There had been little traffic. We made it to Ramsey in no time, a feat hastened by Rich's speed. We pulled into the Clarks' driveway. Rich bolted from the car and toward the house. Barbara and Dave were waiting just inside the front door. Dave shook Rich's hand and before they had a chance to say a word to each other, Barbara threw her arms around Rich and started to cry. "I am so sorry, I am so sorry," she said.

"It's going to be okay. I still believe we are going to find him," Rich said, trying to relieve her.

I was lagging behind a bit, grabbing the jackets and waiting for Michael, who had taken his sneakers off during the car ride and was now fumbling with the laces. As Michael and I walked up the path from the driveway to the house, I could see Barbara with her arms around Rich, and Dave standing next to them. As much as I was eager to get inside and to hear the full story, to listen for details that might yield any hint of Huck's whereabouts, I didn't want to pass through the front door and face another emotionally intense moment. I was too drained. I wanted to get past it. But I also knew how much Barbara loves us all and how hard this was for her and for Dave. I knew they were blaming themselves. I knew, too, they were still wounded from the loss several months earlier of one of their own dogs, Roxroy, a ninety-pound golden retriever, a present from Dave to Barbara shortly before Darian was born, who had died of bone cancer.

Michael and I walked in. Dave leaned down to Michael's eye level, looked him straight in the eyes, and said, "I'm really sorry."

"It's okay," Michael said, as he reached to put his arms around Dave.

I could feel the tears welling inside me. "I'm so sorry, Jan," Barbara said.

We both started crying as we hugged.

"I'm sorry, too," I said. "We never should have put you in this position."

"Of course you should have," Barbara said, abruptly pulling away from me. "I'm your sister. Where else should you have left Huck but my house?"

It was the kind of banter reserved for siblings, the overly sensitive kind that sounds more like a squabble, but it was actually a moment of some release. My saying we should not have put the Clarks in the position of having no choice but to take Huck for a week sounded to Barbara's ears like a criticism. We had now gotten past the moment.

Darian came running down the stairs with an 8½ x 11 inch piece of paper in her hand. She hugged Michael and showed him the sign she had made. Huck looked up from the bottom of the page. Darian and Dave had apparently found the e-mail with Huck's picture and were able to put it on the flyer. REWARD screamed from across the top of the page. But there was no mention of the amount of the reward.

"Darian, the sign is terrific," Rich said, looking at it over her shoulder. "And I'm really glad you found that picture of Huck. But we have to mention the amount of the reward—$1,000. It will get people's attention. It will make them look closely at the sign and take down our phone numbers."

We all went into the kitchen to start to plan our search. We agreed we needed a lot of publicity. Tomorrow's priorities were obvious—get the word out, get the flyers up, talk to people. The goal was to get people in Ramsey and the surrounding towns talking about the runaway puppy and the bereft family. We knew our success or failure was completely dependent on the kindness of strangers.

Dave already had a map of Ramsey spread out on the table. He showed Rich the direction Huck had run and where Dave thought we ought to look. Rich tried to take it all in, tried to avert his eyes from the bodies of water and acres and acres of woodlands shown on the map. The area was more threatening than he had remembered. He tried not to imagine Huck as prey for wild animals, something I had already been thinking a lot about.

I asked Barbara if she had anything Michael could eat. "Of course. What would he like?"

"Mom, I'm not hungry. I just want to go out and start looking for Huck."

I wanted to start looking, too. It was getting so late, I thought we should take our flashlights and go out and ride around and call to Huck. Maybe, just maybe, fate would be kind and Huck was nearby and would respond to the familiar sound of our voices. It was worth trying.

Rich and Dave moved from the map to the computer, making some changes to Darian's sign. They added the $1,000, and the words *heartbroken boy* and printed out about twenty copies.

Barbara volunteered to stay at the house in case any calls came in from someone who might have seen one of the signs Dave and Darian had posted that afternoon. Rich drove, Dave was in the passenger seat giving directions, and Michael, Darian, and I were in the backseat. We started driving up and down the side streets off Wyckoff Avenue. The streets were lit only by the occasional streetlamp. Most of the houses were completely dark. It was as though the entire town was already in bed and asleep.

We parked a few blocks away by the Hubbard school, a neighborhood elementary school, and, flashlights in hand, got out of the car. The only sound we heard came from the empty metal flagpole. The wind was blowing the hooks against it. We started walking around and calling into the darkness, "HUCK, HUCK, HUCK." We'd walk a few feet and call again, "HUCK, HUCK, HUCK." Michael was crying, calling frantically to his lost friend. HUCK, HUCK, HUCKIE. "Mom, we have to go into the woods. He's probably in those woods right there," he said, pointing to a group of spindly-looking bare trees.

I walked with him toward the trees. We took a few steps past the first several trees and shined our flashlights into the velvety blackness. We saw nothing. Michael called again, "HUCKIE, HUCKIE, HUCK, it's me."

But there was no sign of Huck, no movement of any kind.

"Let's go to the hotel and get some sleep," I said, "and then, once the sun is up, we can come back."

"I can't go to bed if Huck is still lost," Michael said.

"If he's out here, that means he's done a good job of protecting himself all day long. He's probably found someplace to lie down for the night," I said. "We'll have a better chance of finding him if we're rested."

I called to the others. Michael and I turned our flashlights off. Michael stood there, staring into the darkness. Then we headed for the car and a night's sleep.

CHAPTER 9

RICH DID NOT need an alarm clock. He had not so much slept as napped, tossing and turning, lying awake, thinking through what needed to be done the next morning, trying to arrange the tasks sequentially in his mind.

The room was pitch-dark, the way hotel rooms with double layers of curtains can often be, even in the middle of the afternoon if the curtains are closed. There was a glow from the clock on the nightstand between the two beds. Rich stared at the clock at 1:00, at 2:30, and again at 4:00, when he considered getting out of bed and heading into town, but didn't. Now it was 6:00, and he was out of bed, fumbling in the dark for his clothes, his wallet, the car keys, and his cell phone.

I had a similar night, waking constantly, worrying about Michael, and wondering if it would not have been a better life's lesson for Michael, albeit painful, to have come to terms already with the fact that Huck had run away and we would never see him again than to set him up for the heartbreak of false hope.

"Are you okay?" I asked Rich quietly.

"I'm going into Ramsey to start looking," he said. "I'll put up some signs and see if there is anyone outside. There just might be someone on their way to work or school who I can talk to. Maybe someone has even seen Huck."

"How am I going to meet you if you have the car?" I asked him, feeling very much like I wanted to get in the car and go with him if it were not for Michael sound asleep in the next bed.

"When Michael gets up, call Dave and ask him to come and get you both. We have to let Michael sleep, and then he's going to need to eat something."

"What about you?" I asked. "When are you going to eat?"

"I'll get something to eat along the way. I want to get going. You might as well try and get some more sleep, because there isn't anything you can do right now. I'll leave you two of the flyers. When Dave picks you up, ask him to take you somewhere where you can get copies made."

"Should we get color copies? They might be very expensive. If we're really going to blanket the town, which

I think we should do, we'll probably need to start with five hundred flyers," I said. I wasn't so much asking him as just thinking it through.

"We have to get color copies; otherwise the flyer won't stand out," Rich said. "If it is in black and white, people will just pass it by," he continued. "The color makes it stand out. Oh yeah, see if you can get tape, too, and a box of plastic sleeves for the flyers we put up on trees and telephone poles. If we don't somehow put the flyers inside plastic, when it rains, we'll lose the flyer."

Rich was obviously way ahead of me. "Okay, that's a good idea," I said. It was so like Rich to think through what would happen to the flyers if it rained or if a good, stiff wind came along. He had an unusual ability to be so singularly focused, to think through many of the details of something, no matter what the distractions were.

"We're just going to have to do what we have to do right now and worry about the money later," Rich said. "We have to be as aggressive about this as we can. I gotta go." He was out the door before I had a chance to respond.

I was too agitated to try to go back to sleep. I took a shower and got dressed, unplugged my cell phone from its charger, and, holding the phone in my hand, sunk into the beige easy chair next to the windows, waiting for Rich to call and Michael to wake up. I realized I had been abdicating much of the planning to Rich. That was unlike me. But I was so focused on Michael, his sense of loss, and how best to comfort him, I couldn't think about much else.

| | |

Outside, Rich pulled out of the hotel parking lot and headed toward Ramsey. The road into town was desolate. It was full of hairpin turns and not much else. Stopped at a light, glancing at the flyers on the seat next to him, Rich remembered he had to find some tape to put the flyers up. He thought about stopping at the Clarks' house once he got to Ramsey, but it was just after 6:00, and they probably would not yet be awake. Just as he decided against stopping at the Clarks, he saw across the road a red-shingled building. There was a wooden sign out front, painted black. In the middle of the sign was a big red strawberry, surrounded by white letters: ELMER'S COUNTRY STORE. There were two gas pumps outside the store and several cars parked in the lot. It must be open. It was.

Elmer's had an old-fashioned lunch counter with chalkboards listing the daily specials. At 6:30 in the morning, the air was thick with the smell of bacon and coffee. The place was full of commuters, truck drivers, teachers, and students, grabbing a quick cup of joe or a couple of fried eggs. Local gossip was traded; newspapers, lottery tickets, cigarettes, and candy were being sold. And on that cold Friday morning in March, a man desperate for a roll of tape successfully talked the reluctant clerk at the register into selling him the only tape he had, the one used in the store, for $2.00.

In no time, Rich was in Ramsey, driving down Wyckoff Avenue, past the Clarks' house, making a left onto Pine Street, the area he thought Dave had pointed to on the map the night before. He parked at the corner, looking up and down the street as he got out of the car. He began walking down the middle of the block, carrying the flyers under his arm.

One clapboard house was nothing like the one next to it. Colonial houses stood alongside split-levels and ranch houses. More often than not, there were multiple cars in the driveways. Each house had a telltale sign about the people who lived inside. Flags, with sayings like "Welcome Friends," or "Grandkids Spoiled Here," hung next to front doors. On some porches, logs were piled high while on others empty rocking chairs sat waiting for spring. Some of the yards were hidden behind fences with a BEWARE OF DOG sign stuck in the ground. In other yards, there were trampolines.

Rich wasted no time trying to get as many people as he could to befriend him and enlist them in the army of people we needed to find our puppy. He stopped the first person he saw, a man in a hurry, dressed in a business suit, who was heading out his front door and down his driveway toward his car that was parked at the end of it. Rich tried to smile. "Sir, do you have a second?" He then recited a quick synopsis of our story and asked the man if he'd take a flyer and tell his friends.

"I'm looking for my son's dog, a toy poodle named Huck. He ran away yesterday morning from my sister-in-law's house on Wyckoff Avenue. My son is heartbroken. We're desperate to find Huck. I wonder if you'd take a look at his picture and call us if you see him. We're offering a $1,000 reward. And please, would you spread the word?"

The man responded readily. "Sure. I'll take a couple of your flyers. That's too bad. How long has the dog been missing?" he asked.

"About twenty-four hours."

"That's not too long yet. I hope you find him," the man said. He then got into his car and pulled away.

The streets in this area off Wyckoff Avenue were labyrinthine. They were full of odd curves and turned in on one another. Rich would cover as much territory as he could on foot and then, before getting lost, go back to the car, drive to another of Wyckoff Avenue's tributaries, park the car, and walk some more.

As the clock passed 7:00 A.M, there were a lot of people leaving their houses, braced for the cold in winter coats and colorful scarves. They were all amiable enough, but all in a hurry. It took only one or two encounters for Rich to develop an ability to surmise how pressing each person's hurry was, and he would adjust his retelling of the story accordingly.

Rich talked to a man named Dan, a woman strapping a toddler into a car seat, and another piling four girls into an SUV. There was a man, whose bathrobe stuck out from under his tan trench coat, who was holding a cup of coffee in one hand while starting the car for his wife with the other. He lived next door to a man in sweat clothes, just back from his morning run. Rich shook hands with everyone he saw, beseeching strangers to deliver his message to their friends. He was starting to feel like a candidate running for political office.

On Forest Avenue, he spotted a pretty teenage girl of about fifteen or sixteen, with dark eyes, dark hair, glasses, and a soft smile. She was about to get into a car driven by a woman who was more than likely her mother. Shy, but eager to help, Kim Romans took a handful of flyers. "I can give them out to some kids I know at school," Kim said.

Kim had a lot of friends at school. She played the flute and the oboe and was the music coordinator for the school's marching band, which competed rigorously each year in the state's competitions. As a freshman, Kim had been a cheerleader, but by her sophomore year she was spending more time with the band, hoping to become its drum majorette.

When she got to school that morning, Kim taped a few of the flyers to the brick wall in the band room and handed others out to friends in classes throughout the day. In cooking class, she gave one to Ray Leslie, a saxophonist and good friend, a boy who kept a fifteen-pound Flemish Giant rabbit named Dante in his bedroom and who volunteered a lot of his time for organizations like Save Darfur. "This looks like something you'd do," she said as she handed him a flyer.

After Kim and her mother had pulled away, Rich continued down the backstreets, thinking how grateful he was to Kim, how unspoiled and sweet-natured she seemed. She had been so approachable and had taken on the task of helping him in the most matter-of-fact way. He walked back to the car, eager to move on to the next neighborhood. Between Kim and the other people he had already met that morning, he was beginning to feel less alone, and it was still early.

Rich drove farther into the maze of streets. Lost in thought, he wandered far from where he had spoken to Kim. The houses were starting to look different. They sat on bigger lots and looked as though they had been built into the woods. The bare trees towered over the houses.

At the end of Stone Fence Road, a cul-de-sac, was a large house set deep in the woods. A barnlike garage sat at the end of a long driveway. Rich watched as a sparkling black Jaguar pulled into the driveway. A balding, sturdy-looking, middle-aged man in aviator glasses with a wide-open face and a compact build practically hopped out of the car.

Harris Rakov had been an attorney in private practice before he decided he had had enough. He traded life behind a desk for life behind the wheel of expensive cars with high-paying clients in the backseat. In his second career, Harris chauffeured people around, listening to their tales and spinning some of his own. Many of his clients flew into Teterboro airport on private jets and wanted to arrive at their final destination in style. In fact, Harris called his new business "Ride in Style."

But mostly, Harris made the incongruous career change because his children were grown and he wanted to spend more time with their mother, whose own schedule as a real estate agent was flexible. Barbara Rakov—a tall, lithesome woman with bright green eyes and delicate features who in middle-age still looked as though she were taking the ballet classes she had enjoyed as a girl in Sheboygan, Wisconsin—was the love of his life.

Harris and Barbara first met at a Christmas party in New York City. She was still living in the Midwest at the time, but had come east to the city for a visit. He wooed her for more than a year until she finally quit her job and moved.

On a frigid January day, just after the calendar was

turned to 1980, Harris took Barbara to the top of the World Trade Center for a romantic dinner. He ordered champagne. He picked up a glass of the bubbly to hand to her, discreetly dropping a diamond ring into it, and asked her to spend the rest of her life by his side. Twenty-three months later, their first child, a daughter, Sara, was born. They brought her home from the hospital on Christmas Eve and set her bassinet down under the Christmas tree.

Harris adored his wife. He kept every note and every greeting card she ever gave him. He had an innate understanding of how tenuous life can be. His own father had died when Harris was only three years old. His mother had raised him in Manhattan, not far from where we live.

Harris was the kind of man who drew people in, rather than turning them away. So when he saw Rich walking toward him, he stretched out his hand before Rich uttered a word.

"Morning," he said.

"Hi," Rich responded. "Do you have a minute?"

"Sure, sure," Harris said. "What can I do for you?"

"Well, I hope you can help me." Rich pulled out one of the flyers and somehow sensing Harris's capacity for appreciating life, gave him the long account of our saga, the one that included cancer.

As it turned out, Harris had had his own brush with children and pets and heartbreak. Some years earlier, his daughter Sara's Russian Blue cat, Little Lely Bluesparkle Rakov, a completely domesticated feline with no claws, walked out of the house. Sara's brother, Nicholas, then a newly minted driver, had backed his car into someone else's, and in the ruckus the cat wandered away.

"It was terrible," Harris explained. "Sara was away at college. We did just what you are doing, we tried everything. Barbara went to the Humane Society, we posted pictures, we left food out for the cat, and Barbara even created a mailing list for every house in the area."

Rich asked the question he wasn't sure he wanted the answer to. "Did you find the cat?"

"You won't believe it. After about six or eight weeks, the cat came home. It was pretty amazing. I came driving down the driveway and there she was, eating the food we had been leaving out for her. I'll bet Barbara would be happy to create a set of labels for you, and you could mail these flyers you have here to homeowners all over the area."

Buoyed by the kindness of a complete stranger's unusual offer of help, Rich thanked him profusely. The two men exchanged telephone numbers. Harris also gave Rich Barbara Rakov's e-mail and work number, so he could be in touch about the mailing list. "I'll tell my wife the story, and you call her a little later, once she's had a chance to get to work and start her day."

Harris and Rich shook hands. Harris turned and headed toward his front door.

As Rich started walking away, he turned back to look at Harris, hoping never to forget the face of this kind man. "Thanks again, thank you so much," he shouted.

"I'll bet you find your dog," Harris shouted back, advising: "Give it some time."

Back in the street and back in the car, Rich could not remember how to get out of the web of streets and back to Forest Avenue. He wondered if this wasn't exactly what had happened to Huck—Huck started into the woods and, before he knew it, was so deep in he couldn't find his way out.

The streets were more deserted now than they had been when Rich set out that morning. Talking with Harris had taken more time than he realized. It was now close to 8:30. For a while he saw no one. He wondered if everyone who was leaving for school or for work had already done so.

That is when he noticed an attractive, petite woman in a brown suede jacket walking a black-and-white Tibetan terrier. Rich pulled the car up alongside the woman, who introduced herself as Lorraine Sassano and her dog as Baxter. Rich asked Lorraine if she had seen a small, red poodle and then told her the story.

"Let me have some of those flyers," she said. "You have to get the word out fast. I work in Allendale. I'll put some up for you," she volunteered. "I'll also put some up in the office I work in. It's a doctor's office, so we get a lot of people in and out who live in the area."

"That would be great. Thank you so much," Rich said, and he handed her some flyers.

"Why don't you try and go to the schools, get a posse of kids together," Lorraine suggested. "Kids like a challenge. If the schools will put up some of the flyers, I'll bet some of the kids will come out to help."

With Kim in mind, Rich thought Lorraine was on to something. Schoolkids probably knew all of the area's hiding places; they probably knew the woods better than most adults. After all, kids went a lot more places on foot and by bike than adults did.

"That's a really good idea. I'll try it," Rich said.

"There is one other thing you should tell your son to do. Tell him to pray to St. Anthony," she said. "He's found a lot of things for me."

"Thank you, I will," Rich said.

Lorraine pointed the way back to Forest Avenue.

So many people had been so nice, Rich now felt emboldened, ready to take his campaign one step further. He had decided to start ringing doorbells at houses where it looked like people were home and awake.

Back on Forest Avenue, Rich spotted a few workmen milling around a colonial house with an American flag hanging off the porch. There was a truck in the driveway, J.H. MYER GENERAL CONTRACTOR, in neat letters across the side. He headed for the front door and rang the bell. John Myer opened the door and stepped outside, his dog, Lily, a brown-and-white King Charles spaniel, following behind him. "Wait, your dog just got out," Rich said the minute he saw the dog come through the door untethered.

"She's okay, she won't go anywhere," John said nonchalantly as Lily lay at his feet.

Rich was momentarily envious that John Myer's dog just lay down on the lawn instead of running away or disappearing into the woods. *Why can't Huck do that?* he thought to himself. He introduced himself to John and told our story while handing him a flyer, realizing as he did that he was running out of copies.

John was a confident man, not just confident that his dog would stay at his feet, but confident in his own skin, a man with an easy manner, a ready laugh, and a firm handshake. A carpenter by trade, the father of three girls, he invited Rich inside, offering to photocopy the flyer.

Rich followed John into the house, through the kitchen, where beautifully tooled cherrywood cabinets lined the walls and a cooking island stood in the center of the room. Off the kitchen was a den, where John's handiwork was on display—thick crown moldings, a wooden mantle above the brick fireplace, a window seat. Off the opposite side of the kitchen was John's home office. Without thinking, John made a fistful of color copies of the flyer and handed them to Rich.

"I'll keep some myself and put a few on the trees and telephone poles on the street. I'll also post them in our trucks and ask my men to keep an eye out," he said to Rich.

"This is really helpful," Rich said. "I didn't realize I was starting to run out."

"Not a problem," John said. "We'll look around. Good luck."

❙ ❙ ❙

While Rich was out walking the streets, and while Michael slept, I took the local phone book from the desk in our hotel room, grabbed my reporter's notebook from my bag, and went into the bathroom where I could turn on a light without waking Michael. Doing nothing was torture. I had to start working the phones.

I sat on the edge of the cold, white porcelain tub, balancing the phone book on my lap, and started looking for the names of local newspapers and animal shelters. I found at least three newspapers we could run ads in. I used my cell phone, which I had held on to since Rich had left, and started calling to find out how to go about placing the ad, and what it would cost. We had done such a good job on the flyer that it would be best if we could simply reproduce it in a quarter-page or half-page ad.

My first call was to the *Suburban News*, a small

weekly paper covering the towns of Ramsey, Waldwick, and Mahwah I spoke to a woman named Pat who said it was too late; the paper was closing that morning. I pushed, trying to see if there was any give at all in her decision. I told her it was an ad offering a reward for information about a lost dog belonging to a twelve-year-old boy. I told her we were from New York and staying in a local hotel, combing the area in search of the dog. I was prepared to tell her the whole story, but I didn't have to. She was persuaded and quickly relented. "If you can get a jpeg file to me in two hours, I'll be able to get it in. But it has to be within two hours."

"That's terrific. Thank you so much. I'll get it to you. Let me take down your e-mail address. And if you hold on, I'll get my credit card and give you the number."

I put the phone, my pad, and the phone book down on the floor. I opened the door of the bathroom to go get my credit card and was startled. There stood Michael, completely dressed, asking: "Mom, can we go? Why did you let me sleep so long? Let's go look for Huck. Where's Dad?"

"Let me just finish on the phone and I'll fill you in on what's going on."

I gave Pat my credit card number and thanked her again. I had no idea what a jpeg file was, but assumed Rich would know and would also know how to send it to her. I walked out of the bathroom and sat on

Michael's bed. He sat down next to me and leaned his head on my shoulder.

"Dad left very early to try and talk to people on their way to work or to school. We wanted to let you sleep because you're going to need a lot of energy today. I was waiting for you to wake up before calling Uncle Dave and asking him to come get us and take us to get more signs made. Then we'll catch up with Dad. Now how about we order you some breakfast while we wait for Uncle Dave?"

Michael wanted to get going but agreed to have some breakfast while we waited for our ride. He seemed much better physically for having had a night's sleep and was more himself, though his characteristic spark was missing. I called Dave and asked him to come and get us and then called room service and ordered Michael scrambled eggs, chocolate milk, and toast. After it was delivered, Michael sat on the edge of the easy chair, leaning over the breakfast tray on the ottoman in front of him. He didn't turn on the television looking for *SportsCenter* and baseball news the way he ordinarily would have; he just sat there, forcing himself to eat a bit of breakfast.

While he did I sat at the desk and called the Bergen County Animal Shelter to find out what happened if someone turned in a lost dog. "If a town thinks there is a lost animal, they'll call us for animal control," the man who answered the phone said. "We'll come and pick up the animal and bring the animal here. We hold them for seven days."

Scared to ask, but going ahead anyway, I said: "And then what happens?"

"We put them up for adoption."

Relieved, I told him our story and asked his advice. "You can come down and fill out a report and look over the dogs we have here," he said. "But quite honestly, I don't remember seeing a dog like that. Why don't you keep looking and come down in a day or two."

It seemed like a reasonable suggestion. The journalist in me had to ask the next question, but I was reluctant to do so because of Michael. He was sitting right there, finally rested and finally eating something. I didn't want to start his day off the wrong way. I didn't want to upset him, but I knew I had to ask "And what happens if a dog is killed by a car or a wild animal and someone finds the dog's body?"

"Well, people will usually dispose of the body; you know, someone in the town will usually be called to dispose of it. We won't hear about it," he said.

I could not help myself. I wanted to be sure I grasped fully what he was saying. Huck was so much a part of who we now were as a family, his constant love such a source of comfort and joy, I found it impossible to believe that he could be killed and no one would tell us. So I asked again, making sure I was getting it right.

"You have been very helpful, sir," I said. "Let me just

make sure I have this right. Are you saying that if our dog or any pet for that matter were killed by a car or a wolf or a coyote, and someone just disposed of the body, we would have no way of knowing?"

"Yes, that's right."

"But what if the animal had tags on his collar with identifying information?" I asked.

"Someone might call you or whomever. But that would just be out of the goodness of their heart. There is no routine in place."

I thanked him and hung up the phone. Mercifully, overhearing the question about finding the dead body of a pet did not seem to upset Michael in the least, or if it did, he didn't say.

I pulled the phone book onto my lap and started thumbing the pages for numbers of other animal organizations that might prove useful. It was hard to tell from the names whether or not they had anything at all to do with finding lost dogs. There was the Humane Society, the Ramapo Bergen Animal Refuge, Animal Control, the ASPCA. It would take a while to call them all. I jotted down the phone numbers, thinking I'd have a chance to call them one by one, as time permitted throughout the day.

l l l

While we waited for Dave to pick us up, Rich had headed for the high school, following up on Lorraine's advice to enlist kids in our search. On the way, right after the curve in Wyckoff Avenue where the road work had been going on the day Huck ran away, on the side of the road ahead, underneath a blue spruce evergreen tree towering above a grouping of smaller pine trees, he saw a large sand-colored stone about the height of a five-year-old child. There was a silver apple on the sign and the words YOUNG WORLD DAY SCHOOL.

Rich parked the car in the school's lot, took a lost dog flyer off the front seat, and went inside. He stood just inside the double glass doors for a minute, listening to the sweet sound of young children's voices accompanied by a piano. "I've Been Working on the Railroad," their voices growing louder and more jubilant when they got to the chorus "fi fie fiddly-i-o."

It was warm and bright and cheerful inside those doors. It was a refuge. There were bulletin boards on the pale yellow walls, each filled with a brigade of white snowmen fashioned from the children's imaginations and put up against a blue background. Below the bulletin boards were rows of pegs, and hanging off each peg was a backpack. Above each classroom door was a welcome sign. Rich felt a bit like an intruder, and in an era when men are viewed with suspicion when they are around children other than their own, he wondered how he would be received. "Excuse me, I wonder if I could speak to the person in charge?" he asked the middle-aged woman behind the desk, who was cheerful and did not seem the least bit bothered by his request.

"She's tied up right now, but if you'd like to sit and wait, she should be free in about ten or fifteen minutes."

Rich was still thinking about the kindness of strangers, when the person in charge materialized, seemingly out of nowhere. Janet Jaarsma sat down next to Rich and listened intently while Rich once again related our saga to someone he had never set eyes on before.

Janet had been at Young World, a school for children as young as two years old that goes through fifth grade, for decades, making real her vision of a school with an emphasis on the positive, on what children can do instead of what they cannot. The warm, calm feel of the school that Rich felt as soon as he stepped through the doors was her indelible stamp.

Janet grew up in an era, she later described, as one in which "children were seen and not heard." Her girlhood days were spent in the quiet community of Prospect Park, New Jersey, where she walked to school five days a week and to church on Sundays. As a teenager she volunteered some of her time at the local hospital, Paterson General.

She was a petite woman with graying hair. She had

been raised with the expectation that she would work hard, do well, and use her considerable talents to help others. She did. She completed both a bachelor's degree and a master's degree at a time when women were less likely to do so than they are now. Janet married a man named Richard with a passion for literature and who shared her can-do, independent approach to life. They raised two children.

Janet had a soft touch and a reverence for good manners and beautiful flowers. Sitting on the small bench-like seat next to the one Rich sat on, she thought he seemed quite distraught and tried to calm him by drawing him into the compassionate ethos of the school.

"I have always felt that if everyone bends their minds and hearts to a task, then good things will come," she said to Rich as he sat there, stunned that this woman was so welcoming and so generously using her time and her energy to help him. "Let me take a look at the flyer."

She took one look at the picture of Huck and smiled. "Here's what we'll do. I'll make a large copy of this flyer and put it in the windows out front. When people drive by or when they come here to pick up their children, they'll see it," she said. "If anyone connected with the school has seen your dog, I am sure they will help."

For Rich, it was the latest in a series of extraordinary acts of kindness by people who, without thinking twice, interrupted their day to give so freely of themselves. Everyone, even the people in a hurry, stopped and gave Rich their time, responding in whatever way they could to his plight. No one shut the door or turned him away. To a person, Ramsey was opening their hearts to Rich and by proxy to us.

Back in the car, Rich thought he ought to get to the other schools as quickly as possible and pursue the idea of a posse of kids. It was Friday, so if he did not reach kids today, he would not have another opportunity until the weekend was over. Driving back down Wyckoff Avenue toward Main Street, Rich, one of the most die-hard New Yorkers imaginable, a born city boy, was beginning to appreciate life in a small town. He was taken by how willing people were to give him the great gift of time. Most of the people he had talked to that morning had not made him feel that he had to tell them our story in a hurry. Like Janet Jaarsma, people seemed so open to giving him whatever amount of their time it took for him to explain our situation. It was such a contrast to life in New York, where a moment too long spent deciding on a bagel topping while ordering it in a deli could get you pushed aside in favor of a more decisive customer.

But Rich did not allow himself to bask too long in the warmth of all the compassion extended to him. The hours were passing and Huck had not been seen. Not one of the wonderful people who were sympathetic to our tale had seen Huck or knew of anyone who had seen Huck. There was no telling if he were even alive.

Rich forged ahead, hoping that what he was doing was laying the foundation for our publicity drive, which would keep the eyes of an entire community looking in the woods for Huck. He drove past the sloping lawn of Ramsey High School, parked the car in the lot in the back, and found his way to the principal's office.

Mrs. Maxwell, a kind woman with a shy demeanor, said the principal was not in and suggested Rich discuss his desire to put signs in the school with someone over at the Board of Education. Those offices were housed in a stone building just behind the high school.

Rich hurried over. Just inside the door sat the receptionist, Annette Augello, a diminutive woman with dark eyes who had been sitting there, surrounded by children's artwork, greeting people, for fifteen years.

"No, no one is in right now who could give you permission for that kind of thing," she said.

Frustrated, Rich feared a descent into bureaucracy. The distance between his charged manner and Annette's placid one was increasing. Annette asked Rich if he'd like some water and led him into a nearby conference room. Pictures of the town's schools hung on the paneled walls; there was an American flag in one corner and a television hanging from the ceiling in another.

In the center of the room was an enormous oval table with upholstered chairs pushed underneath it, taking up most of the floor space in the room.

Annette and Rich each pulled out a chair and sat down. Rich took a sip of water from the plastic cup Annette had handed to him and then tried to explain to her how important it was that he be allowed to put up a few signs right away in the school. He handed a sign to Annette, hoping she would be moved. But she was unyielding. She said she simply did not have the authority to say yes or no.

Trying to be helpful, she offered that there was a community service club in the high school that might be willing to help. It was now after 10:00. She suggested Rich call her later in the day and she would try by then to have an answer about the signs and the club.

I I I

At the same time Rich sat in the offices of the Ramsey Board of Education, worrying that he had hit a dead end, I was at a Staples store near the hotel with Michael and Dave. We were waiting, while an older, heavyset woman wearing a red smock made us five hundred color copies of the flyer. We had found the tape and the plastic sleeves. When she finished, she handed the stack to Michael and told us to pay at the register. "Are you the heartbroken boy in this flyer?" she asked Michael. Before he had a chance to answer, she said: "I'll give you one piece of advice: Pray to St. Anthony. If you do, you'll find your dog." Once again, a stranger had suggested praying to St. Anthony for heavenly help in finding our lost dog.

Michael was nonplussed.

"Thank you," I said, answering for him. "We will."

We paid as quickly as possible and headed for the car. I called Rich and told him that we had to move quickly to get the ad in the local paper. We agreed to rendezvous back at the Clarks' house, so Rich could use their computer to send the jpeg file. It would also give us a chance to figure out our next move. The charge in Rich's cell phone was starting to run out and he was afraid to stay on the phone very long. Despite being frustrated at the Board of Ed, Rich was excited about the progress he had made in the hours since he had left our hotel room. "It has been a great morning," he said. "I'll fill you in when I see you."

"Did you meet anyone who has seen Huck?" I asked.

"No, no, but I met a lot of good people who are going to help us." I know it was terribly unfair, but I got off the phone wondering how Rich could possibly say it had been a good morning if he had not in fact met a single person who had seen Huck. It was a good thing Rich had been the one to go out in the morning and start meeting people. I was entirely too edgy and too sure that in the end I'd be the one to comb every corner of Ramsey looking for Huck. I suppose in that moment I had less faith than Rich did that people we didn't even know would actually want to help.

"Where are we headed?" Dave asked.

"Back to your house."

"Did Rich have any luck this morning?" he wanted to know.

"He says he had a great morning and met a lot of people who will help us," I said. "But he also said he did not see Huck or meet anyone who had seen Huck, so I have no idea what to think."

"Mom, do you think I should pray to St. Anthony?" Michael asked.

"It could only help," I said.

The truth was, I didn't know what to say.

CHAPTER 10

BACK AT the Clarks, after the jpeg file was successfully sent to the *Suburban News*, Rich, Dave, Michael, and I stood in the kitchen, leaning our backs
against the edge of the counters, catching each other
up on the events of the morning and deciding how to
divide the next set of tasks. No one was relaxed enough
to sit, even for a few minutes. It was getting near eleven
and the day was slipping away.

After hearing about the idea of a posse of kids, Dave
suggested we go to another area high school—Northern
Highlands—in nearby Allendale. He walked over to
the kitchen table where the map was and showed Rich
how to get to the school.

Dave had a couple of business appointments, so he
was going to be unavailable for a few hours, which also
meant we would be down to one car. I offered to walk

up and down Main Street and ask the merchants to put the flyers in their shop windows. Rich said he and Michael would go to the Ramsey police station and then to Northern Highlands.

Michael, the only person to have gotten any sleep at all or to have had anything to eat, although he had not eaten much, was eager to get going. "What are we standing around for, let's go," he implored.

We headed out to the car. I asked Rich to drop me at the top of Main Street. Once there, I set off with an arm full of posters and a bag full of tape. "Mom," Michael called to me, "make sure they put the sign in a place where people will really see it."

"That's good advice. I will," I called back to him.

"Good luck."

"Good luck to you, too."

My first stop was a deli and convenience store, creatively named The Store, advertised in a bright green-and-white sign above the double glass doors. It was a place where just about anything anyone might need was packed into seven short aisles. A cup of coffee or a freshly made sandwich could be had anytime day or night.

A neatly dressed man named Unmesh had bought the store a half-dozen years earlier after coming to the United States from England to join his large extended family in New Jersey. Like so many of the people in Ramsey, Unmesh was civic-minded, allowing local charities to put their collection bins for used clothes in his parking lot. When I asked him if I could put one of our flyers in his window, he took the tape from me and put it up himself, separating it from the other home-made signs touting piano lessons, landscaping services, and babysitters.

"We want to be sure people see this one," he said.

I wasn't sure if Michael had phoned ahead or if St. Anthony was already intervening, but I was grateful Unmesh had thought to display the flyer so prominently, just as Michael had hoped.

"I see you have a lot of signs in your window," I said. "It is really nice of you to help people out."

"If it helps somebody, we want to do it," he said. "It's a small thing."

It was not a small thing to me. We shook hands. I felt like I had scored an early success. If everyone was as nice as Unmesh, Huck's picture would soon be in every store window in town.

I crossed over to the other side of the street and went into the redbrick post office. Inside the door was a bronze plaque: UNITED STATES POST OFFICE JOHN F. KENNEDY, PRESIDENT OF THE UNITED STATES, 1962.

Nineteen sixty-two was exactly what all this was beginning to feel like. Walking up and down Main Street, despite the circumstances, had some of the charm of a bygone era—the open, welcoming attitude of the people, the slow tempo of the day, the unencumbered feel of things.

There was a bulletin board in the post office, like Unmesh's window, filled with homemade posters and business cards advertising services of one kind or another. Roofers, travel agents, garage organizers. One sign had a picture of three perfectly erect dogs on it, a German shepherd and two golden retrievers; it was advertising dog training services. TEACH YOUR DOG TO STAY BY YOUR SIDE, it read. I took a stray tack and put our flyer next to it, hoping someone who saw it would appreciate the irony.

The movie theater took a flyer and put it right up in the ticket window. The hair salon took three. The bagel store took two. The hardware store put one in the window and a stack by the register.

In the middle of Main Street was a store I had passed in the car many times on visits to the Clarks, but never really knew what it was. There were two planters out front at either end of the large storefront window. In the window, heavy, colorful striped drapes were held open with tasseled fabric ropes revealing a big red wooden cabinet with oddly connected merchandise piled high—a wooden table, a watering can, a canister, two toy rakes, a stone penguin. I stopped and took a close look through the glass front door.

I stepped through the doorway and into a fairy-tale sugarland and was greeted by the owner, John Crames. He was a man with big hands and hair cut like a marine, a man who used to own car washes. He had created

LoLo's because he wanted to run a business with his wife, a business that made people happy. "I like candy. I like the way it looks. It's like we're a bar," he said. "When you're sad or you're happy, you come here."

LoLo's is no ordinary candy store. Along the walls are all manner of candy to scoop into a bag and buy by the pound—chocolate gummy bears, chocolate krispies, chocolate pretzel poppers, and sour watermelons. Under a glass case with an American flag sticker on it are truffles—butter toffee, Irish coffee, white Russian, and black forest. Then there are chocolate pizza-making kits, books on cupcakes, cookies in the shapes of baseballs and basketballs. There is a tree of lollipops. When I commented on the unusual array of goodies in the immaculate store, John said, "If I can find it in the mall, I don't want it in my store. We try to sell things you can't find anywhere else."

He offered up his delectable treats, but I politely refused. It was too early for chocolate and I probably did not have the stomach for it at that moment anyway. I told him our tale and he recounted his own, involving his dog Otis, an Akita pal from his bachelor days. John had left Otis in someone else's care while he went to Florida. A medical emergency arose. Treatment did not come soon enough and Otis died. John didn't say how long ago it was, but it was clear in his telling of the story that the pain of the loss was still close to the surface.

"Why don't you go ahead and put one of your flyers

up there on the bulletin board," John said, pointing to a bulletin board near the front door with the words LOLO'S TOWN CRIER above it. "People stand around eating candy and reading whatever is up on the board. People will read it. They'll see that cute picture of your dog, and they'll read it."

John's story about Otis turned my mind back to Huck. As kind as everyone was, it was incredibly draining walking in and out of stores, repeating our story, asking for permission to use their store window as a billboard. My stamina was waning. I was committed to our plan of publicity, but I was starting to have more and more doubts that this intense effort was actually going to yield anything. Shouldn't we be out driving around looking for Huck?

After saying good-bye to John, I was back on the sidewalk, walking past the gas station. I had been canvassing the area for more than an hour and wanted to sit down but I wouldn't allow myself the respite. There was a lot of territory to cover. Results, the exercise studio, took a couple of flyers; so did the video store. Next to it was Pet-A-Groom, a store devoted solely to the grooming of the town's pets. Just as I opened the door to walk in, a young woman holding a thick red leash with a perfectly coiffed collie on the other end was walking out. She spied the flyers in my hand. "Did you lose your dog?" she asked. "I'll take one of your flyers and put it up at my church. I'm on my way there now."

"Thank you so much," I said as I handed her a flyer.

She held it in her hand, taking a few seconds to read it, and then looked up at me and asked: "What happened?"

I filled her in as quickly as I could, not wanting to appear anything but thankful for her help, but it was hard to mask my sense that time was disappearing and talking to her was eating up precious minutes. She must have realized my sense of urgency because she brought the conversation to a close, saying, "We'll pray for you."

Inside the pet store were bulletin boards filled with pictures of well-groomed cats and dogs—on the beach, in front of Halloween pumpkins, there was even one of a dog sitting on Santa's lap. It was like being in a pediatrician's office, only with pictures of terriers, retrievers, and mutts instead of children. I was always wary of people who had crossed the line and completely anthropomorphized their pets. And although I kept telling myself I was nowhere near that line myself, owning a dog as an adult, I saw how easy it is for dogs to become peoplelike members of the family. I had not yet put Huck on Santa's lap, but it was not totally out of the question either. I was hoping I would still get that chance.

Doreen Tietjen didn't worry about such boundaries. Franky, short for Champion Robbans Four Seasons, was her prizewinning rottweiler, also known as "her girl," but only one of many animals she had raised and loved. This was her store. She presided there like a devoted schoolteacher over her charges. "I know who they are the minute they walk in," she said of the animals left in her care.

Doreen was a self-proclaimed tomboy, a fierce competitor while growing up, who had an unusual feel for all inhabitants of the animal world, including the kind most of us have a hard time warming up to, like snakes and turtles. She'd find them in the woods and bring them home.

When she was ten years old, her parents enrolled her in horseback-riding lessons. Before long she was carefully tending to the horses, keeping up the sheen on their coats, and with her mother behind the wheel, hauling them around in a trailer attached to the back of the car to horse shows where she often walked away with a ribbon or trophy.

By the time she graduated from high school, she was a pro. But the family's fortunes were unstable, and though she wanted to go, she could not afford college. Nor could she afford to keep on riding and showing horses. She married at nineteen and divorced at twenty-one.

Doreen held life and limb together with a series of jobs—she was a liquor store manager, she studied and became a wine sommelier (finishing first in her class), and she worked in a computer store. But each of those posts was wrong. She longed for the connection nurtured in her as a child, the connection to animals.

One day, fate and a boyfriend took her to the Westminster dog show at Madison Square Garden. It changed her life. She loved being around the dogs. She loved the tension of being a competitor. Six months later, she bought her first show dog.

She did not stop there. Dogs began to take the place of horses in her heart. She wanted to be near them every day. She enrolled in the Nash Academy for Dog Grooming in Cliffside Park, New Jersey, and after six hundred hours of apprenticeship and little else, had the temerity to open her own grooming store in Ramsey.

Doreen was immediately sympathetic to a family in search of a lost dog. Our connection to our dog did not have to be explained. "Let's put up a bunch of signs; we'll put a couple in the window and a few around the store and one in the back where we groom the dogs," she said.

I asked her, based on her experience, if she thought someone might steal Huck and bring him to a groomer to change his look, as Lisa, the breeder, had suggested when I called her from the airport in Florida.

"Nothing like that would happen around here," Doreen said. "But it is possible someone would find him and not be able to figure out how to reach the owner and eventually bring him in here. We will all keep an eye out. You know people around here are pretty good about things like this. If anyone finds your dog, they'll make an effort to get him back to you."

"That's good to know," I said. "What do you think happens with runaway dogs most of the time, really?" It was the question I kept asking, hoping for some kind of assurance, something to stifle the gnawing uncertainty that we might ever see Huck alive again.

"Well, I think most of the time the dogs eventually find their way home, but your situation is different because your dog ran away from a place that is not his home," she said in a straightforward manner. "It is hard to know."

I appreciated her honesty, even though it was not the least bit reassuring. Picking up on my undiminished level of anxiety, Doreen said: "Listen, I'm happy to help you in any way I can. Just let me know. Here's a card with our number on it. Call if you need anything at all. If I'm not here, the girls here know how to reach me."

I I I

A few blocks away, Michael was arriving at the police station with Rich and feeling some of what I was, a sense of desperation about the way we were spending our time. He was grateful, too, but with every offer of help, Huck seemed farther and farther away. Michael hoped to find some answers at the police station.

As father and son walked together over the mat that said WELCOME TO THE RAMSEY POLICE STATION, Michael had some trepidation, wondering if there might be prisoners inside and what he, a twelve-year-old boy, was doing there. It felt just a little bit scary.

Inside was a small waiting area. There were a few metal chairs and a counter topped with a smoky glass divider that reached the ceiling, behind which were several desks and a television. The concrete brick walls in the waiting area were filled with plaques, all testaments to the police department's tireless work in caring for the town's well-being. There was one from Don Bosco Preparatory High School, a local Catholic school for boys. The plaque was identical to one posted in the school gym as a "lasting tribute to all the men and women who daily risk their lives in the line of duty."

There was a plaque from the county in recognition of Ramsey's dedication to victims of domestic violence, a reminder that even this bucolic little town struggles with darkness.

Most of the plaques, though, about a dozen or more, had to do with the police force's involvement in the state's Special Olympics. The largest of these plaques had a three-dimensional torch on it. The plaque read:

> Every year thousands of law enforcement officers run
> throughout New Jersey carrying the Olympic torch—
> or flame of hope—to spread awareness of the abilities

of children with mental retardation and other closely related developmental disabilities.

Rich went over to the glass divider and explained to the police dispatcher sitting on the other side of it in front of a console why he had come. "That's a tough break," the dispatcher said. "Why don't you have a seat and I'll notify an officer."

While they sat waiting, Michael and Rich started talking about what it takes to spend your life serving others in the way police officers do. They talked about all the brave policemen and policewomen in New York who had lost their lives on September 11. Before the conversation got much further, Michael and Rich were ushered into a back office. There were no prisoners in sight. A tall, burly, round-faced police lieutenant appeared. There was something about him that was both comforting and intimidating. "What can I do for you?" he asked.

After hearing the story from Rich, the whole story of our runaway dog, Lieutenant Mark Delhauer sprang into action. He said he'd alert the entire Ramsey force and he'd go one better. He'd radio all the police officers in neighboring towns. He'd use the flyer to give them a description of Huck and tell them to be on the lookout. He said he would also post it in the squad room so the officers on all shifts would see it. Michael was beginning to feel hopeful. Finally, some real help. A man with power, with a true ability to mobilize a lot of people was going to help us.

Rich asked Lieutenant Delhauer the same thing I had asked Doreen. "What usually happens in cases like this?"

"Ninety percent of the time, the people get their dog back," he said confidently.

"Thanks very much for all your help" Rich said, as he extended his hand to the officer.

"You're very welcome," Lieutenant Delhauer said, returning a firm handshake. And then putting a hand on Michael's shoulder, he added, "We'll do everything we can."

Walking out of the police station, back over the welcome mat, Michael turned to Rich: "He was really nice. This is the best I have felt yet."

But Rich, while comforted, had his own nagging worries, one of which was raising Michael's hopes, while also preparing him for the possibility that we might never see Huck alive again. "I liked him, too," Rich said.

"Ninety percent is a high number," Michael said.

"It is. Those are good odds," Rich responded, but then cautioned: "Keep in mind, though, Huck did not run away from his own house, he ran away from a house he is not all that familiar with. That could lower those odds a bit."

Michael's newly found high spirits were undiminished. Lieutenant Delhauer had inspired him. Michael was now a full partner, committed to fanning out, getting our flyer before as many eyes as we could. He was ready for Northern Highlands High School.

As Rich and Michael drove through the winding streets on their way to the school, Michael's eyes kept searching the wooded areas for Huck. The trees were still bare, which was a blessing. The woods were so dense that seeing into them would have been just about impossible if it had been spring or summer and the foliage full.

"The principal is not available for a while," the secretary in the high school administration office said to Rich and Michael. "Would you like to meet with the assistant principal, Mr. Occhino, who could see you now?"

Rich and Michael looked at each other and said "Yes" at the same moment.

Joe Occhino, a stocky man with an athletic build, a quick smile, and an intense look in his eyes, invited Michael and Rich into his office. They took in his impressive collection of Yankees paraphernalia—hats, balls, signs—sitting on a shelf above his desk. Turns out, twenty years earlier, Joe had ventured to the Yankees' team tryouts in Florida to try his luck. In the process of showing off his skills, he had managed to break a bat belonging to Graig Nettles, the legendary third baseman.

But alas, Joe did not become a professional ballplayer. Before becoming assistant principal of Northern Highlands High School, Joe had been a physical education teacher, a baseball coach, and a guidance counselor. He had an unflinching belief that "you will only be remembered for the person you are and the lives you touch," as he told Rich and Michael on that cold afternoon in March.

His only regrets had to do with the children he could not help, who somehow passed through his school unnoticed or unreachable. The part of his job he never expected, the toughest part of his job, was weathering the loss of kids taken from this earth, teenagers who got behind the wheel of a car drunk or went careening down a black hole after experimenting with drugs.

Prominently displayed on his desk was a photograph of a young blond boy walking down a dusty road with a dog. In large letters was the word GUIDANCE. Underneath it, "For our children, the road to happiness and success is usually paved by our example."

The walls and tabletops were filled with tokens from students whose lives he had affected. They vowed to never forget the teacher who had helped them navigate the rocky shoals of adolescence.

Two girls who had recently graduated had left a plaque behind. It said:

Mr. Occhino, A Special Person.

    In the world there are few people who are truly special. They go around caring for others before themselves. They have a smile on their face and love in their heart for everyone. They ask nothing in return. I see all this and more in you.

Rich and Michael knew they were sitting in the office of a man who understood children. They imagined he had a light touch with his students, able to reprimand without damaging self-esteem.

As Rich spun out our story, Joe kept looking at Michael. "I'm moving this to the top of my priority list," he said to Rich and Michael. He said he saw sadness in Michael's eyes. Joe decided in that moment that everything else he had been doing that day had to come to a stop.

He asked the secretary in the outer office to make a hundred color copies of the flyer. "I'm going to give these out in senior study hall," he told Rich and Michael. "And then I'm going to the cafeteria where right now about half the student body is eating lunch. These kids like to help people. These are the kind of kids who gave up having a day off on Martin Luther King Day to work in a soup kitchen."

After a quick good-bye and an exchange of handshakes, Joe moved quickly through the school library and upstairs to a classroom full of seventeen- and eighteen-year-olds, many of whom welcomed the interruption to their studies. "What's it worth, Mr. Occhino?" one of the boys asked Joe.

"You find this dog and you won't have to serve detention for the rest of the year," he promised.

Joe then went to the cafeteria and personally handed out all but a few of the remaining flyers, which he taped to the walls by the school's main entrance. As he did, he thought about Brandy, the small dog, half sheltie and half miniature collie, beloved by his daughters. When the girls were young, Brandy had squeezed under the fence and run away. The young family's frantic search had turned up no trace at all of Brandy. Night after night, Joe left the gate open, hoping the dog would find her way home. Three days later, on a Saturday morning, Brandy walked through the open gate and stood barking at the back door. Like the storied Lassie, Brandy had found her way home.

Outside Northern Highlands High School, on his way back to the car, Rich tried to reach Annette Augello to see if any progress had been made over at Ramsey High School. His cell phone kept dropping the connection.

He and Michael drove back into Ramsey, with Michael again searching the woods with his eyes for any sign of Huck. "Let's go find Mom," Rich said to Michael. "Let's see how many signs she was able to get posted in Ramsey."

On the way to Main Street, they saw a sign on Wyckoff Avenue for the Hubbard School, the school whose grounds we had searched in the dark the night before.

"Let's see if people in this school will help us, too," Rich said to Michael. "Then we'll find Mom."

The school was set far back from the road. They drove down Hubbard Lane, parked the car, and eagerly headed toward the front of the yellow one-story brick building. The flagpole, whose empty hooks had clanged against the steel pole the previous night, was now festooned with an American flag, snapping in the breeze. They walked past a row of bicycles, some spanking new, others finely aged, none of them locked, many with helmets hanging off the handlebars.

Rich and Michael were shown into the principal's office. Michael E. Gratale had a bowl of Hershey kisses on his desk. He was a short, powerful-looking man, with a graying beard, a former woodworking and mechanical drawing teacher who had spent most of his decades-long career in the Ramsey Public School system.

Before Michael had a chance to sit down next to his father, the principal asked him to wait outside. Rich thought it odd. And what happened next was even odder. Once Michael left the room, Mr. Gratale leaned across his desk, looked at Rich, and asked: "Okay, what is really going on here?"

In very measured tones, Rich explained our predicament.

"I understand now," the principal said. "I could sense your distress when you walked in and I just wanted to be sure everything was right about this situation. I see a kid not in school and a distraught man and I have to wonder," he said. "But I understand now what is going on. This is surely one special dog. We'd be happy to put up one of your signs. "

Rich thanked him and left a sign, collected Michael who had been sitting in the outer office, and headed back outside to the car. The air was starting to warm, and Rich took a minute to take a few deep breaths.

"Why did that guy throw me out of his office?" Michael asked.

"Well, I guess they are not used to having a father and his son walk into their school in the middle of the afternoon and ask for this kind of help. Maybe they thought we were up to no good. It may have all seemed strange to him, and he didn't want to ask me about it with you in the room," Rich said.

"That sounds really crazy to me, Dad."

"Well, it was a little crazy," Rich said, now starting to see the humor in the exchange with the overzealous principal. He started to laugh.

"I mean, what did he think?" Michael continued. "That you were some kind of weird guy or something?" And now he, too, started to laugh.

"How could anyone be scared of you, Dad?"

CHAPTER 11

I HAD BEEN at it for hours. In the past hour alone, I had been to the hardware store, the gas station, the nail salon, the pizza shop, the florist, the meat market, and Shanghai Gourmet. All of the shopkeepers were sympathetic, all took flyers, and all wanted to help. Many people told me their own harrowing tales of runaway pets. Anyone who walked down Main Street now could not get from one end to the other without feeling as though they'd seen Huck's picture everywhere.

Tired and thirsty, I finally sat down on a bench. I called Rich and Michael to confer about our next step. They were not far from where I was on Main Street and said they had enlisted more help, met some fantastic people, and were on their way to pick me up.

Soon after, they pulled up right by the bench and I stood up wearily, pulling my bag behind me. Just as I got into the car, Rich's cell phone rang. He was hoping it was the woman from the Board of Education getting back to him as she said she would.

"Hi, my name is Tina. I just saw your sign at Young World. I think I saw your dog."

Rich was thunderstruck. "Oh my God—where? Did he look okay? When did you see him?"

"I saw him sitting by a mailbox on West Crescent, just sitting there, yesterday afternoon, while I drove my sons home from school. I thought it was strange that such a young-looking puppy was just out like that, by himself. He is such an unusual color; you couldn't help but notice him.

"I just saw your sign now at Young World, so the boys and I came home and got cream cheese and went back over to West Crescent to see if we could find him again. We looked around. He wasn't there."

"Did you happen to get the house number?" Rich asked.

"I don't know the number, but there is a curve in the road, and a green house with kind of a swampy pond next to it," Tina explained. "There is a mailbox by the driveway, close to the road. That's where I saw him."

Rich, who by now had reason to believe most people in town would do anything to help us, didn't think twice before asking Tina if she would mind meeting us where she had seen Huck, just to be sure we went to exactly the right spot. Without hesitating, she agreed.

Rich hung up and pulled out a map Dave had given

him earlier, repeating to Michael and me the details of his phone call while he checked and double-checked the location of West Crescent Avenue. "A woman saw the sign at Young World and called to say she had seen Huck. Unfortunately, it was yesterday afternoon," Rich quickly explained. "But it is still a sighting."

"Let's go. Let's go," Michael yelled from the backseat.

I was astounded. I don't know which surprised me more, that someone had seen both Huck and the sign and had gone to the trouble to call us, or that Huck was alive as of yesterday afternoon. I echoed Michael's excited scream, "Let's go."

Rich's phone rang a second time. This time it was Ray Leslie, the boy in Kim Romans's home ec class. "Did you find your dog yet? 'Cause if you're still looking, I have some time and I can help you look."

"That's incredibly nice of you. We're just heading to West Crescent where someone saw Huck," Rich said.

"Okay, I'll catch up with you at some point," Ray said.

With both hands on the wheel, Rich sped down Wyckoff Avenue. He turned right onto West Crescent, a heavily wooded street with houses set far back from the road. Just where the road winds sharply was a two-story, blue-green house with a big bay window and a low stone fence lining the long driveway leading up to it. The house's side lawn sloped down into Van Gelder's Pond, a marshy-looking body of water filled with bramble. To the side of the driveway's entrance, at the point in the road where cars have to slow in order to safely take the curve, was a mailbox, the mailbox where Tina had seen Huck sitting forlornly twenty-four hours earlier.

Rich parked the car at the end of the driveway. Just then, Tina drove up with three of her children in the backseat. Without getting out of her car, she motioned toward the mailbox. "He was sitting right there," she said. "You might ask the people who live there if they saw him. Call me if you need any more help. You have my number now in your cell phone."

Rich, Michael, and I stood looking down at the pond. Unspoken, but understood, was the terror that Huck, whose instincts were still those of a puppy, still not fully developed, might have mistaken the branches and leaves clouding the water for solid ground and tried to walk on them, or lost his footing at the pond's edge while trying to drink. I was nearly paralyzed with fear.

After a moment, I started down toward the water, stepping carefully. Soon I was ankle deep in leaves, though still on solid ground. It was just about impossible to see tracks of any kind of animal, let alone those of a small dog. I stood looking at the dead body of water trying to assure myself that dogs, even young ones, instinctively avoid danger in the natural world. Maybe they'd run into traffic, but they wouldn't fall into a swamp.

Protecting Michael from what might have been a

slippery slope, from the danger of the water and the fear of what we might find there, Rich took him and headed toward the house. They climbed the stone steps and rang the bell. No one was home.

We met back at the car. "There was no real reason to think Huck would still be here," Rich said as we all got back in the car. "But the one thing we learned was that as of yesterday afternoon, which was about eight hours after he ran away, Huck was still alive. That was an important phone call."

Rich was right; there was no reason to think we would find Huck still sitting by the mailbox on West Crescent Avenue. We had, though, been so euphoric that someone had responded to our flyer, that someone had actually seen Huck, that we had gotten our hopes up in a way that was out of proportion to the slim news we had received. We were now deflated.

We headed back to the Clarks' house to see if either Dave or Darian was home yet. There is strength in numbers, and we knew we needed more boots on the ground.

When we got there, we found them both home. Dave still had the map spread out on the kitchen table. Rich stood next to Dave, pointing to where Tina had seen Huck. Dave took a pencil and marked the location of the mailbox. As he watched Dave draw an X on the map, Rich realized that the streets he had spent so much time walking during the early morning hours, the ones where he had met Kim, and Harris, and Lorraine, were all on the opposite side of Wyckoff Avenue, far from where Tina had seen Huck. The thought that he might have wasted the morning only made him more anxious.

The day was disappearing. It was late on Friday afternoon, about 4:30 or 5:00. All we had accomplished was getting the word out, getting the flyers around. It had taken an enormous effort and had yielded only one phone call, a lead that was too old to be meaningful. It was hard to rally and it would soon be dark.

Rich had been in motion all day, not allowing himself the time to sit down and have a meal. He had not had a minute to collect his thoughts or figure out what he was going to tell Michael if our worst fears were realized.

As he moved toward the kitchen sink to get a glass of water, his cell phone rang. He barely said hello when a frantic voice at the end of the phone screamed: "We just saw your dog. If you go right now, you'll find him. He's standing in the woods with another dog. Go to the woods on Deer Trail. Go now!"

"Thank you, thank you so much!" Rich yelled into the phone. And before he had a chance to get her name, or tell her that if we found Huck, the reward would be hers, she hung up.

"Dave, do you know how to get to Deer Trail? Huck is there right now!"

"Sure. It's not too far. Let's go in two cars," Dave said. "Janet can ride with me. You take the kids and follow us."

"Michael, Darian, come on," I yelled to them. "We just had another call. Get in the car. You can both ride with Dad."

They came dashing down the stairs, nearly falling over each other. We all ran out of the house, knocking over a small table and a green-and-white ceramic vase near the front door.

As I jumped in the car with Dave, I actually allowed myself to believe we were about to find Huck. I could not imagine another emotional plummet. Part of me, too, was drained. I needed my family intact again. I wanted to be home in our small apartment playing one of our favorite family games, Apples to Apples, with Huck sitting at our feet. I wanted a hot shower and a decent meal. I wanted to sleep in my own bed and linger over coffee in the morning. I wanted to take Huck for a walk in Carl Schurz Park and watch the tugboats on the river. I wanted this nightmare to end. I thought it was about to.

But from the road, there was no sign of Huck. We parked. As we got out of the cars, a group of about six kids, all around the age of thirteen or fourteen, all on bikes, approached us. "Are you the people who lost the dog?" one of them called to us.

"Yes, we are," Rich said. "Have you seen him?"

"No," the boy on a blue-and-silver Mongoose bike said. "But we came out to look."

"That's fantastic," Rich said. "We just had a tip from someone who said they saw him around here."

"We'll ride around and look." And before he and the other boys pedaled away, one of them, a boy in a hooded black jacket, asked, "If we find him, do we get the reward?"

"Definitely!" Rich said.

The band of bikers took off.

To get to the dense woods, we first had to climb a hill. There were no clear paths into the woods. We decided to split up. Rich would take Michael and Darian in one direction, and Dave and I would go in the opposite direction. Rich and the kids were ahead of us. As I watched them disappear into the thickly packed, bare trees, I realized dusk was beginning to set in.

"Dave, I'm going to go back to our car and get a couple of flashlights," I said. "Do you want to wait?"

"I'll just start into the woods, but I'll go slowly, so you'll be able to catch up to me."

Not wanting to lose a minute, I summoned the energy to run down the hill, raced for the car, grabbed the flashlights, and ran back up the hill. As I started to walk into the woods, I called to Dave who heard me and called back, but he was out of my line of sight. Rather than spend time trying to find him, I shouted to him that I'd go it on my own.

The air had grown cold again. I started walking, the sticks and underbrush cracking under foot. "HUCK, HUCK, HUCKIE," I called again and again. None of us had heeded our own advice to strangers about the cream cheese. In our rush to get to the woods, we had left it behind. "HUCK, HUCK, HUCK, HUCKIE" I kept it up. My tone was loud, and by now, pleading.

Rich, Darian, and Michael had crossed a stream, slowed only by Darian's momentary apprehension. They were now deep into the woods, also calling out for Huck.

Realizing nightfall was only minutes away, Dave found his way back out of the woods. He called Rich on his cell phone and told him to get the kids out, that soon it would be dark, and since it was overcast, there would likely be no moonlight to guide them.

While trying to retrace their steps and find their way back to the road, Rich heard my plaintive calls for Huck and saw me before I saw him. Standing there watching his wife, only months out of cancer treatments, wandering the woods in the cold and near darkness, screaming for our lost dog, he began to feel bad that he had led the family to believe that this could be done. Maybe the whole enterprise was taking too much out of all of us and sooner rather than later it was time to come to terms with a very harsh reality.

I knew I had to get out of the woods, and as I turned in the direction of the road, I spotted Rich and the kids. I gave Rich a flashlight, he took it and my hand, and sidestepping rocks and branches of trees, with Michael and Darian trailing behind us, we made our way out of the woods, without Huck.

"Are you okay?" Rich asked. "I'm worried about what this is doing to you."

"It is taking a toll on all of us. But I'm okay," I said. "Really." And then I said what we both already knew. "In a way, these sightings are making it harder. It is impossible not to get your hopes up and then the dis-appointment is devastating. It is a real emotional roller coaster. It is tough enough for us, but I hate doing this to Michael and now Darian."

Dave was waiting by the cars. In his usual unassum-ing way, he suggested that as long as we were in this particular area, we ought to look in the vicinity of the golf course, a few blocks away. He had to head home, but before he did, he explained to Rich how to get to the golf course and said he thought we should also look on the street that borders it, Carriage Lane. I drove so Rich would be free to look at the map and direct. Dar-ian and Michael, whose high hopes had been so cruelly dashed, were sprawled across the backseat, thoroughly exhausted.

As I fastened my seat belt, Rich looked at me. "You know, we can pick this up tomorrow. We don't have to go to the golf course. Or I can take you back to the Clarks and I can go," he offered.

"No, I'm fine. Let's all go," I said. I felt better about actually looking than I did about putting up signs and asking people to be on the lookout and to spread the word. It just felt more productive. I felt closer to Huck.

We drove through the dimly lit streets, down Shady-side Road, left onto Pine Tree Road, right onto Hemlock Road, left onto Carriage Lane.

And then, all of a sudden, there stood Huck.

"THERE'S HUCK!" I screamed. There he was on Carriage Lane, just walking slowly down the middle of the street as though he'd had a long hard day. I stepped on the brakes, pointing the car away from him so the headlights would not scare him. Huck stopped, turned his head, and looked right at us.

"There he is, there he is!" everyone in the car screamed all at once.

There was no time to discuss the best way to handle this. "Michael, you go," I said. "Call to him; when he hears your voice he'll come."

Michael crawled across Darian to open the car door nearest to Huck. He got out and before he even had a chance to take a step toward Huck or call his name, Huck took off. "HUCK!" Michael cried. "HUCK! HUCK! COME BACK!"

"Michael, get back in the car, quick," Rich said. "He can't outrun the car. Let's move it."

Michael jumped into the car and slammed the door shut. I sped the car down Carriage Lane. But Rich was wrong. Huck did outrun the car. He ran right into a wooded area at the end of the dead-end street. There was a house nestled in those woods. I pulled the car over to the side of the road. We all leapt out of the car and ran up the endless driveway of this house and into the woods. The light coming from the porch was not enough to allow us to see into the black thicket of trees. "HUCK, HUCK, HUCK," Michael, Darian, Rich, and I cried out again and again. But Huck had disappeared into the night.

Michael stood staring into the woods. I put my arm around his shoulders. "I want to go into the woods. Let's use the flashlights. Please, Mom. I don't think he's far away."

I stood next to Michael and turned on the flashlight, shining it into the woods. "You can't really see much. And if we go into the woods, we're liable to meet up with other animals, and we'd probably get lost. It's not a good idea."

"But we can't just leave," Michael pleaded.

"I'm afraid we're going to have to," I said. "But we'll be out again as soon as it is daylight. I promise."

"HUCK, HUCK, HUCK, HUCK, COME BACK," Michael screamed, his face red with emotion. "PLEASE."

Darian joined him. "PLEASE HUCK, COME BACK."

This was exactly what both Rich and I had been worried about from the outset, that the heartache would only get worse. "We better go, kids," I said gently.

"No, I don't want to go," Michael said, even as he turned to walk reluctantly toward the car.

We all headed back to the car in stunned silence. Without missing a beat, Rich summoned strength and hope I did not have. "I know we didn't get him, but we know he is alive; that is the most important thing," Rich said, then turned to look directly at Michael and Darian in the backseat. "We now know that he can make it through a night."

I I I

From the road, we could see that most of the lights were on in the Clarks' house. It was a welcome sight.

"I saw Huck," Darian said excitedly to Dave and Barbara as we walked into the house.

"You're kidding! That's fantastic," Barbara said, at the same time searching Rich's face for an explanation of how we could see Huck and now be standing in her kitchen without him.

Rich recounted our sighting and Huck's flight, masking his own disappointment in the telling.

Hearing the story, with Michael and Darian waiting to hear her reaction, Barbara said she saw it as a step in the right direction. "Even though you didn't catch him, you know he's still okay. And I have more good news. While you were out, six people called to say they had seen Huck. SIX!" she said. "All of them saw Huck earlier in the afternoon, but at least people are seeing the flyers."

Rich jumped in. "That's good," he said. "But there is a problem here. People are seeing the posters hours after seeing Huck. It means the publicity is lagging behind the sightings." He added, "We have to get more signs out and we have to do it faster."

Rich and Dave then walked into the kitchen and stood over the map, like two generals in a war room. Dave had marked the location of each of the sightings and he and Rich tried to figure out the path Huck had been on.

Barbara, Michael, Darian, and I stood looking at the map, too. Dave pointed out Carriage Lane and the Darlington County golf course that bordered it. Beyond the golf course was an open expanse of land, which on the map looked like something to be measured in miles rather than acres.

"What's this?" Michael asked, pointing to the green mass on the map.

"It's the Capgaw Mountain County Reservation; it's a state park," Dave said. "There are hiking trails and ski runs there."

"I'll tell you one thing, if Huck goes in there, he ain't never coming out," Michael said in a way that suggested a note of finality as he walked out of the kitchen.

After reconstructing Huck's movements, Rich called Michael back into the kitchen in an upbeat tone. "Listen, Mikey, I'm feeling really good right now and here's why. Look at this path Huck has traveled," he said, pointing to the map. "Have you ever learned in school about something called the law of disorder, some people call it the random walk theory?" he asked.

Hanging on Rich's every word, Michael shook his head no.

"It was a theory developed by Albert Einstein that says that if you blindfold someone and tell him to walk, he will keep passing back through the place where he started, no matter how many times he changes direction."

"Really?" Michael asked.

"Now here, look at where Huck has walked. He has crossed over his own path a couple of times."

"Is that really true?" Michael asked. "Couldn't the person just keep moving away from where they started from even if they don't move in a straight line?"

Rich was saved by his ringing cell phone. It was Ray Leslie wondering if the tip we had gotten that afternoon had helped us find Huck.

"No, Huck is still missing, but remarkably we actually saw him. We just weren't able to catch him," Rich explained.

"Then he's still missing and you still need help?" Ray asked.

"Yes, Huck is still missing and we still need a lot of help," Rich responded.

Ray said he was sorry he had not caught up with us that day but would be out there first thing the next morning.

Rich hung up the phone and momentarily put his head on the table, on top of the map, closing his eyes for just a moment. I went and stood next to him, and sensing my presence, he reached up and put his arm around my waist. "We did a lot today. We'll go at it again tomorrow," I said, trying to let him know that I was where I knew he was—exhausted but not about to quit.

Rich stood up and started to fold the map while Dave set the table for dinner. Magically, Barbara had managed to make chicken and salad and Michael's favorite, her signature mashed potatoes. We all sat down to eat.

CHAPTER 12

WHEN WE LEFT the Clarks' house around nine
o'clock that night, the air felt even colder than
it had the night before. I could see my breath. I had to
wear gloves. The temperature was already below freezing, below 32 degrees, or it would be soon. How much
cold could Huck withstand?

Back at the hotel, the mood in the lobby was festive. A boisterous wedding party was gathered at the
bar, probably having just finished the rehearsal dinner.
There was a black baby grand piano in the middle of the
lobby and a man of about fifty sat at the keyboard playing and crooning. "Will you still need me, will you still
feed me, when I'm sixty-four."

Up in our room, the mood was decidedly not festive.
Two overwrought parents tried to put on a good front
before getting their child into bed. Michael had held on

to Rich's explanation of the random walk theory and found some comfort in it before drifting off. That was not true of Rich.

Once Michael was asleep and the lights out, Rich allowed his own fears and worry about never finding Huck—random walk theory or no random walk theory. He was haunted by Huck's momentary glance in our direction and then his bolting far away from us. While it was heartening to see Huck, to know he was live, his retreat away from us was almost too much to bear. We had found Huck and then lost him again in a matter of seconds. It was a tough end to a grueling day.

"I suppose Huck ran because he was scared of the car, not because he was scared of us or didn't know Michael," I said to Rich.

"That's probably right," Rich replied, comforting us both, whether he believed it or not. "It is too bad we weren't on foot at that point. I think we would have had a better chance. We should also have had some food with us. Let's get some cream cheese tomorrow before we head to Ramsey."

"Let's also get some bologna," I said. "Huck loves bologna almost as much as he loves cream cheese."

Rich and I each had another fitful night's sleep. Despite my physical and emotional exhaustion, I didn't fall asleep for more than a twenty-minute stretch until some time around three o'clock in the morning. Rich was up at daybreak and slipped out of the hotel room without waking Michael or me. He wanted to go back to Carriage Lane, where we had seen Huck twelve hours earlier.

It was Saturday; people were not rushing off to school or work. Rich pulled into the parking lot of the twenty-four-hour A&P just across the highway that intersected with the road our hotel was on. He walked through the automatic doors, past rows of potted plants on risers, past the produce section and the salad bar, to the deli counter. There was no one there slicing meat. Who would want to buy sliced cold cuts at seven o'clock in the morning? To the side of the counter was a refrigerated display of prepackaged meats. Rich grabbed a package of bologna. He wasn't going to risk seeing Huck again without being armed with food. He headed for the dairy section and grabbed a plastic silver container of Philadelphia Cream Cheese. He was the only customer at the only open register. He paid and went back out to the car.

As he drove past Elmer's, Rich did not see a single car in the parking lot. He drove down Ramsey's Main Street, where all the stores were still shuttered, past the Clarks' house, where no lights could be seen from the street, and onto Carriage Lane. He parked and just sat there. The skies were ominous. The streets were eerily still.

Pensive and filled with melancholy, Rich kept going over all that had happened to our family during the past year—the terror of a cancer diagnosis, the arduous months of treatments, the death from cancer of our friend Connie, falling in love with Huck, finally getting a vacation, and now losing Huck. Through it all, Rich had been unfailingly strong and positive. He now felt drained. He had needed that vacation as much as I had needed it. He did not know how much longer he could lead the rallying cry.

He stared into the woods where Huck had run from us and willed Huck to come out again, to give Rich one more chance to bring home our Huck, our indefatigably affectionate best friend, who had, even before he came to live with us, brought us new life, unconditional love, and a renewed sense of fun.

Rich's solitude was interrupted by the ring of his cell phone. It was Ray Leslie, the high school boy who wanted to help find Huck. Rich explained where Carriage Lane was and Ray said it would take him a while to get there, but he'd probably be there in an hour or so.

Rich hung up the phone and sank back into his painful thoughts and torturous remorse at having left Huck in unfamiliar surroundings in the first place. He somehow could not stop blaming himself. In his estimation, he had let his family down and the repercussions would be wounding. His guard was lowered; tears welled in his eyes.

Rich heard another car. He looked in his rearview mirror and saw Dave driving toward him down Carriage Lane. The two brothers-in-law apparently had the same thought. Go back to Carriage Lane and see if by some miracle Huck might still be there. Rich got out of our car and walked toward Dave's. Dave lowered the window, took one look at Rich, saw how moist his eyes were, and averted his gaze for a minute, giving Rich a few seconds of privacy to pull himself into the here and now.

"What do you think, Dave? What do you think is going to happen?" Rich asked.

"I think in a few days he'll get hungry and show up at someone's door," Dave said. It was a supposition that had more to do with his compassion for Rich than what he really believed was in the cards.

The two men stared at the chain-link fence and the golf course on the other side. "Let's go talk to the rangers on the golf course," Dave proposed. "We've got to drive around to the other side of it, which will take us on some busy roads, but there is a chance that Huck could have slipped under this fence and gone onto the golf course somewhere. I think it is worth talking to them."

It was better than sitting in the car. Rich got back

into our car and followed Dave to the golf course. They parked next to each other and then walked toward the one-story white building with a green roof that stood between the parking lot and the entrance to the course. While they did they made small talk, but not uncomfortably so. Rich asked Dave about who used the course. His mood was beginning to pick up. Action always feels better than inaction. Dave's steady manner helped.

That cold Saturday morning in March, the golf course was empty. Even golfers did not feel the lure of the outdoors on this dark day. Inside the squat-looking building was a small pro shop, which was not doing any business. There was also a reception area with a desk where user fees were paid. Behind the desk was a fit-looking older man, probably in his seventies, with silvery hair. Another equally fit man of about the same age was milling around. Dave approached the man behind the desk, giving him an abbreviated version of Huck's disappearance and asking if he'd mind if he and Rich put a few signs up. "Sure, go ahead. But I haven't seen any dogs around here."

Rich, whose only experience with golf was the kind played with brightly colored balls and a single club on a course with obstacles like windmills and streams, said: "When you speak to the rangers, would you ask them to try and apprehend Huck, not just tell us that they saw him."

The two silver-haired men looked at each other. There was a pause in the dialogue.

"Uh, Rich, these are the rangers," Dave said softly.

"Oh, I'm sorry, I didn't understand. We'd appreciate anything you can do—a phone call letting us know you or someone else saw him out here on the golf course would be great."

Back outside, Rich and Dave, whose moods were so weighty earlier, shared a laugh. Rich's naïveté, his unfamiliarity with the workings of the county golf course, his expectation that surely men in charge of so much acreage would be young and muscular and dressed in uniforms, gave Rich a chance for lightheartedness. "Now that is one of the dumber things I've said in a while," he said self-deprecatingly.

Rich headed back to Carriage Lane to wait for Ray, while Dave headed to the hotel to pick up Michael and me. We were already in the lobby when Dave arrived. Michael, downtrodden after coming so close to being reunited with Huck the night before, was wearing the green Yankees cap with the shamrock on it.

"Remember that golf course from last night?" Dave asked as Michael and I got into the car. "You know the one that's on the edge of Carriage Lane? Rich and I went over there this morning. The guys who work over there agreed to put some signs up and to keep a lookout for Huck."

"I don't really think he did go in there," Dave said. "I just wanted to make sure we covered all the bases."

"That was a good idea," I said, almost distractedly, worrying about something else. Rich had been doing too little sleeping and eating. "Do you happen to know if Rich had anything to eat?"

"I don't think he has. I'll bet you and Michael haven't either," Dave said. "Let's stop on our way and pick up some muffins and coffee."

Something about the time spent with Dave, whether it was the laughter or the companionship or the feeling of being proactive, had returned Rich to his determined self. He did not want to waste time waiting in the car for Ray. He wanted to start searching the woods Huck had run into the night before. He drove around to Pine Tree Road so that he could enter the woods from the far end.

Just as he eyed the woods at the end of the block, Ray called again, this time saying he was on his bike today and was riding up and down Carriage Lane. "Oh, you're on your bike," Rich said. "Oh, I thought you would be driving. Ray, how old are you?"

"I'm fifteen," Ray said, altering the mental picture Rich held of Ray.

"Were you on your bike yesterday?" Rich asked.

"No," Ray said. "Yesterday I was walking."

"Ray, I didn't realize any of this. I just assumed you

were old enough to drive. I am only a block away, on Pine Tree, toward the end of the street. Why don't you lock your bike to the golf club fence until later and walk over here."

"Okay," Ray said.

"You can drive around with me and I'll take you back to get your bike later," Rich added.

Ray turned out to be a boy with bright brown eyes, freckles, and a winning smile. He had a sense of social commitment that belied his years, which probably was in part what made the teenager get up early on a Saturday morning to go out and help strangers search the woods for their lost dog. That particular morning Ray was dressed in jeans, a green T-shirt that said SAVE DAR-FUR on it, and a blue parka with a ski lift ticket hanging off the zipper.

Like Michael, Ray loved animals and had to beg his parents for years before he finally got a pet. Reluctant to become dog or cat owners, Ray's parents thought a rabbit would be easier. Along came Dante. They knew Ray would fall in love with his new friend. They did not know they would, too.

Dante was not named for the writer of the epic poem or for the rings of hell. According to Ray, he thought the name sounded spunky and it fit the floppy-eared, domesticated rabbit's personality. Dante lived and grew in Ray's bedroom. He was as affectionate as any lap-dog, happiest when human hands were caressing him. There were a lot of close calls with departure, as Dante repeatedly chewed through leashes and ropes used to secure him in the yard.

As Rich and Ray walked into the woods that morning, Rich learned that Ray was a triplet with a passion for jazz and Gerry Mulligan, the breezy jazz saxophonist.

In the course of getting to know each other, while Rich and Ray were trading the outlines of their lives, they stumbled on the fact that Ray was actually the cousin of one of Michael's classmates. It was an odd coincidence, especially given that Michael went to a small school with only fifty boys in each grade.

Ray, intensely curious about the dog we were working so hard to find, privately doubted that Huck could possibly still be alive. Still, he wanted to help and listened carefully as Rich gave him all of the details of seeing and nearly catching Huck the night before.

"Wow. Well, I sure hope he did not go onto the golf course," Ray said. "There is no place for a little dog to hide out there. It is so open, and at night there are a lot of animals like foxes and raccoons. I'd be scared out there."

The trek through the woods continued. Rich and Ray crossed a stream wide enough to make it impossible to step from one side to the other, forcing each of them to balance on a rock in the middle of the water in order to get to the other side. Rich had been doing so much of this the past couple of days that he did not hesitate for a moment and made the move as nimbly as his new teenage friend. The woods held no signs of life of any kind. If there were any plant shoots pushing through the ground, signaling the impending spring, the brown leaves and broken twigs and branches were not yet letting them through. Rich, with a package of bologna in one pocket and a tub of cream cheese in the other, called to Huck, listened for him, but heard nothing except the sound of his own breathing. "He's not in here," Rich finally said to Ray. "We'd better go back out to the street."

They made their way out to the road. They saw a man standing at the edge of a deep front lawn in front of a cedar-shake-shingled colonial house with a driveway that curved around the side of it.

"Let's go talk to him," Rich said to Ray. "Maybe he's seen Huck."

The man stopped and watched as they approached. "We're looking for a lost dog," Rich began.

The tall, friendly-looking man, Dick Seelbach, and his wife, Jackie, owned two Scotties, one of whom occasionally ran away only to return. These people loved dogs. They had bred, raised, and successfully shown their Scotties for forty years. Dick was a delegate to the American Kennel Club.

So a day earlier, on Friday afternoon, when Dick saw a small, red poodle first in the woods, and then sitting by his neighbor's pool, he kept an eye on him, realizing the dog must be lost. He said he watched the dog for the better part of the afternoon. Eventually Dick tried to catch him.

"But that little guy, he wouldn't let me anywhere near him," Dick told Rich and Ray. "He just took off." It was another sighting, but another one that came too late.

Rich recognized in Dick another new friend ready to support our search. He told Dick our story and explained how warm and welcoming everyone in town had been. He handed Dick a flyer, telling him how we, too, had seen Huck on Friday. "Your telling me that you saw Huck right here all afternoon tells me that we must have seen him right after you tried to catch him," Rich said to Dick. "Geez, we were so close. Thank you for trying."

"There is always a chance he'll come back this way," Dick responded. Rich asked if it would be okay to leave a piece of bologna and a bit of cream cheese at the end of Dick's driveway.

"Sure," Dick said. At which point Ray, who had been silent, wondered aloud if food left out like that would do much good and might only attract other animals like deer, given the proximity of the Seelbach house to the woods. But Rich was not deterred and left the food anyway.

The men shook hands. "Thanks a lot for trying to catch our dog yesterday," Rich said.

"I really hope you find him," Dick said. "I'll keep an eye out for him."

As Rich and Ray continued up the street, past Dick's house, Rich ruminated aloud, "I wonder who else around here saw Huck yesterday. For that matter, I wonder if Huck has been seen around here this morning. Maybe after Huck ran into the woods last night, he came back out into this neighborhood."

It was late in the morning, about 11:00. Rich's eyes darted up and down the street, looking for anyone who might be lifting a grocery bag out of the trunk of a car or puttering around in a yard. He noticed an open garage and an open front door diagonally across the street from the Seelbach house. It was a gray-green colonial house with black shutters and white trim. There was a basketball hoop on the driveway and an SUV parked underneath it. "Let's go talk to those people."

Rich and Ray walked up the driveway and up a step or two to the path that led to the front door. Rich rang the bell. A middle-aged man came to the door and stepped outside. "We're looking for our dog," Rich said as he pulled a flyer from his pocket. "Last night he ran into the woods at the end of your block after spending most of the afternoon in this neighborhood. I was wondering if by chance you had seen him."

"This now makes sense to me," the man, who later

introduced himself as Brian O'Callahan, responded. "Last night I thought I heard something outside. I told my wife I thought it was a wild animal. Then I heard what I thought was the sound of dog tags and I said to her, 'No, it can't be a wild animal, because I think I hear tags. We both thought it must be a dog.'"

"Do you remember what time that was?" Rich asked.

"It must have been around ten o'clock," Brian said. "I'd say in all likelihood it was your dog because dogs around here aren't wandering around like that, off a leash, and out of a yard."

Rich began to give Brian some of the details of our story. He described the events of Friday, putting the pieces together as he did. "If Huck was in your yard late last night, it means he probably never went far into those woods after he ran from us in the evening, or, if he did, he found his way out again. We were afraid he might have gotten through the fence and onto the golf course, but based on what you're telling me, Brian, I think the golf course scenario is unlikely."

Brian wanted to do something. "I will help you in any way I can," Brian offered. "Can you give me something that smells of your son, like a glove? I'll take my sons and our dog and we'll look in the woods."

"That is incredibly generous of you," Rich said, once again at the receiving end of a stranger's kindness. "I hate for you to interrupt your Saturday."

"It is no problem at all," Brian said in a way that made

Rich know Brian was the kind of man used to helping others in the most unceremonious of ways. "You can't be here all the time," Brian continued. "But I am here, so I can be your eyes and ears. Think of me that way. I'll give you all of my phone numbers, every way you can contact me, anytime you need anything at all."

Then he asked: "Who is your sister in-law? Maybe I know her." As it turned out, one of Brian's sons was Darian's age. They were in school together. The O'Callahans did know the Clarks.

Going back over Huck's movements on Friday, Rich was frustrated and now regretted going home once Huck ran into the pitch-black woods that night. It was maddening to think of how close we were to Huck without being able to find him.

Michael and I were still in the car with Dave headed in the direction of Carriage Lane. We had stopped to pick up some coffee and muffins, which, along with a lot of Saturday shopping traffic, had slowed us down. I called Rich to find out exactly where he was. Michael and I were eager to join him and resume our search. Rich explained that he had met up with Ray and they were now at the foot of Pine Tree Road. "Meet us here."

Once there, I left Dave and Michael in Dave's car and took a bag of muffins and a cup of coffee to where Rich and Ray were standing, next to our car, at the edge of the woods. Rich introduced me to Ray, who said he was going to take a few minutes to go back into the woods. I handed Rich the blueberry muffin and put the paper cup of coffee on top of the car.

Rich had a smile on his face as he started to tell me about the latest kind stranger he had met. "You won't believe this guy we just met, Brian O'Callahan. He lives right there," Rich said, pointing to the house, as he broke off a piece of the muffin and ate it. "He said he heard an animal outside his house at about ten o'clock last night. First he thought it was a wild animal," Rich continued, "but then he heard dog tags jangling and realized it had to have been a dog."

He took a sip of coffee. And then went on. "I think that had to have been Huck. Brian is an incredibly nice man. He said he's going to take his kids into the woods to look some more."

As I stood there listening to Rich talk about Brian so enthusiastically, I thought about how easily and deeply moved Rich could be by people who are sincere, and how much he abhorred any kind of feigned sentiment and any kind of snobbery. The people he had been meeting, Brian being the latest, had touched him. I could see already that he had affection for them that I knew would be lasting.

From where we were standing, we could see Michael and Dave in Dave's car. We watched as Michael climbed from the backseat to the front. "Why don't you come up front and have a muffin and some juice," Dave had said to Michael. Michael slid into the seat next to Dave and took a muffin out of the white paper bag on the floor. There was a console between the two seats. Dave pulled something out of the console that Michael could not see.

"I have been driving around with this since shortly after 9/11. A man I hardly knew gave it to me, and when he did, he said I might need it for hope," Dave continued. "I want you to have it."

He extended his open hand to Michael. In it was a white baseball, with red stitching, a symbol of their shared passion. On the baseball in red letters was *09-11-01. Do not lose heart. Corinthians 4:16–18.*

"Really? Are you sure you want to give this away?" Michael asked, touched by his uncle's generous spirit.

"I'm sure," Dave said. "I think you need it for hope."

"Thank you so much, Uncle Dave."

Michael held the ball in his hand. There was something soothing about just holding it—the firm, familiar feel of a baseball, the way it fit in his hand, the way the stitching felt against his palm. It was the comfort of an old friend. He felt optimistic. He put the ball in the pocket of his winter jacket and zipped the pocket closed, opening it many times as the day wore on, taking out the ball, holding it, squeezing it, and then tucking it away again. It was a private moment between uncle and nephew. Neither Rich nor I saw the ball until late that night.

Standing by the car, Rich and I reviewed our options. We were trying to decide between spending more time in the woods looking for Huck and putting up more signs in the hope of having more people keeping an eye out for him.

After some discussion, we decided we had to put up more signs. As hard as it was to leave the spot where we had last laid eyes on Huck, we knew we still needed to reach more people in the community. The challenge we recognized yesterday, that the publicity was lagging behind the sightings, was still a problem.

We walked over to Dave's car to run the idea past him. He seemed to always have another map of the area. He did then, too, and got out of his car and spread it across the hood. "I don't think Huck did go onto the golf course. I didn't see any kind of an opening in that fence that he might have gotten through," Dave said.

"I think you're right," Rich said. "I just talked to a guy who knows Barbara, by the way, and he said he heard an animal in his yard last night at about ten o'clock. He heard dog tags. My guess is that it was Huck."

Dave went on. "I say we head more in the direction of Mahwah. We cross over West Crescent where that mailbox was, where that woman saw Huck on Thursday, and up toward Youngs and the surrounding streets."

Dave knew the area well. I was inclined to do whatever he thought was the right thing to do, but I was concerned that although we had put flyers in just about every retail establishment in Ramsey, we had not put them up on telephone poles or trees, in places people might notice from their cars. Maybe it was more important to do that than to head to Mahwah. But Rich thought Dave was right, that we needed to expand the radius. For now, he thought we ought to get some signs up in the area Dave was suggesting and then we could return to the neighborhoods closer to the center of Ramsey.

We kept trying to make decisions based on facts and logic, and when that failed, on educated guesses. But the truth was, we were mostly flying blind; we had no idea what we were doing. Sure, there was some logic to running ads and putting up signs and alerting people to be on the lookout for a lost dog. But deciding which direction he might have run in?

Rich, Michael, and Ray went in one car. Dave and I went in the other, stopping at the Clarks to pick up Darian and to get hammers and nails. When we pulled into the driveway, Barbara came running out. "Anything?" she asked.

"Not much," Dave said. "Rich talked to someone on Pine Tree Road who heard a dog in his yard at about ten o'clock. So if that was Huck, there's a good chance he did not go onto the golf course, which I don't think he did, anyway."

"What's the plan?" she asked in a surprisingly upbeat tone.

"We're going to put up some signs in the neighborhoods on the other side of West Crescent. If this theory that Rich has is right, Huck might cross back over that area where the woman saw him by the mailbox and he might head up toward Mahwah."

Barbara wanted to get in the car and go with us but held back so she could man the phones in case anyone called. "I'd better stay here," she said. "You know today is a big shopping day; the stores will be crowded. More people will be in places looking at our flyer," she theorized. "Hopefully, someone who sees one of our flyers will see Huck, too, and will call."

I started thinking about the kind of shopping most people do on a Saturday: grocery shopping. I realized I had never put a sign up in the supermarket in Ramsey, probably because it was not on Main Street.

In a panic, I asked Barbara: "Where do most people shop for groceries around here?"

"Probably Shop Rite," she said. "Why?"

"We have to put a sign up there," I answered.

"You mean you didn't put a sign up in the supermarket?"

Typically, she sprang into action. "Get in," she ordered. "Honey, we'll be back in a minute," she called to Dave who was now in the garage searching for hammers and nails.

In full sister mode, while driving to the supermarket, Barbara continued voicing disbelief that I had somehow missed putting a flyer there. "I just can't believe you went to all those stores and didn't go to the supermarket," she said playfully. "What is the first stop every parent makes on Saturday morning after their kid is done playing sports?"

"We live differently," I said in a pathetic attempt to defend myself. "Grocery shopping is not an event. It is something that gets squeezed in after everything else," I said. "On Saturdays, after our games, we go out to lunch, or we walk through Central Park."

"Yeah, I know, you're so civilized and all we do is drive around and shop. I'll wait here," she said as she came to a stop in front of Shop Rite.

I went into the store, noticing a large bulletin board just inside the doors. Shoppers could not miss it as they exited the store. It was around noon, and the store was packed. Supermarkets in the suburbs look a lot different from supermarkets in Manhattan. For one thing, there is much more space. The aisles are wide, the carts are bigger, the inventory is dizzying, and there are many, many checkout lines.

I asked one of the women in a deep green shirt standing behind one of the cash registers where I could find the manager. She pointed to a man in his thirties who was standing politely, while a much older woman was yelling—and I do mean yelling—at him about whether or not the coupon she had presented for paper towels was still valid. She called him "stupid" and told him she was going to get him fired, that he was "not smart enough" to do his job. I thought I would do him a favor and interrupt.

"Excuse me, sir, I am sorry to interrupt," I began.

"Oh, that's okay," he said. "What can I do for you?"

With that, the yeller turned on her heels and walked away.

"Would you mind if I put this flyer up on your bulletin board?" I asked the store manager as I handed him one of our flyers.

He took a minute to read it over. "A thousand dollars—this must be one heck of a dog," he said. "How old is the boy you say here is heartbroken?"

"He's twelve," I responded.

"So it's not so much the dog as the kid," he said.

"It's both," I replied.

"Tough age for this," he said. "My sister's boy is twelve. Why don't you put one up in the front window as well. We're not supposed to allow that, but why don't you go ahead and do it. Today is a busy shopping day. A thousand dollars will catch a lot of eyes."

"Thank you very much," I said. "I really appreciate your help."

I got back in the car and told Barbara how nice the store manager had been. "Of course," she said. "I've been telling you for years, everyone here is nice."

Seizing my opportunity for some sibling one-upmanship, I said, "Well, not everyone. You should have heard this woman yelling at him about paper towels and coupons."

When we got back to the house, Dave was waiting outside. "We'd better go," he said to me. "I told Rich, Michael, and Ray that we'd catch up to them."

"Where is Darian?" Barbara asked Dave.

"She had basketball practice and I told her she should go to that and then she could come back and help us some more," he said. "I think it is important for her to go to practice."

"I agree with you. I'm glad you told her that," Barbara said. "I'll see you guys back here later. Let me know if anything happens."

"We will," Dave replied. "And, honey, call us if you get any calls from anyone saying they've seen Huck since we saw him last night. Anything before that isn't much help."

I was sorry Barbara was staying home. The brief ride to the supermarket together, with our sisterly banter, was a welcome respite from the weight of emotion that had hung over just about every moment of the last few days. I thought our plan to go to Mahwah would be another dead end. I didn't want Barbara to leave, taking with her the chance for some momentary psychic relief. I didn't want to face any more wrenching moments.

CHAPTER 13

D AVE AND I got into his car. He handed me two hammers and a box of small nails.

"Once we get up in that area, I'll stop and we can
both get out and nail the flyers onto as many phone
poles and trees as we can," he said. "I still have a box
of those plastic covers in the backseat, so why don't you
start fitting flyers into the covers while I drive."

I reached into the backseat for the flyers and the
plastic sheaths and started putting one inside the other.
The papers did not slide in easily; the paper stock was
too cheap and the fit was tight, so each one took some
effort, leaving me with fingers full of paper cuts.

We drove up the winding back roads. As we got farther away from Wyckoff Avenue, it became harder and
harder for me to believe that Huck could have traveled
such a long distance. Could Huck really have run all

this way? I was already second-guessing, third-guessing, the decision for all of us to spend precious hours of daylight walking around an area that seemed too far away to yield any results. As we had been all along, we were operating on faith, and mine was shaky at best.

From the car, I spotted one of our posters on a telephone pole, and then another on a tree, and another. Rich and his band had already been here. It was reassuring to see that the signs were clearly visible from a car.

Dave and I drove on past that grouping of poles and trees to another, where we parked the car beside a thick, bare oak, and got out with our hammers and nails and signs encased in plastic. With one hand I used a nail to hold a flyer against a telephone pole; with the other I raised the hammer and began pounding the nail into the dry wood. By the time I drove in the second nail, I thought I was getting pretty good at it, having hit my thumb only twice, my other fingers not at all.

We went on this way for a while. Sometimes Dave and I would both get out of the car, and other times, when there was only one pole or tree, Dave would stop in the middle of the deserted road and I'd jump out of the car and quickly hammer the nails into the sign. From the car, it was easy to pick out the spots that would be in a driver's line of sight.

About an hour or so later, we caught up with Rich,

Michael, and Ray on Fawn Hill Drive. We parked and got out of the cars, once again to confer about the division of labor. I had not had much time alone with Rich, so I proposed dividing into two teams of poster hangers—Rich and I would go in one direction, and Dave, Michael, and Ray would go in the other. There was no resistance.

As Rich and I started walking down the street to-gether, now alone, I asked the unthinkable. "Don't you think we should have an idea in mind of how long we want to keep this up? We've got Michael on an emo-tional high wire, and I'm really worried about what will happen if he falls, and it is looking more and more like that is what *will* happen. We've also got Darian there."

"I'm worried about it, too, but I can't think about stopping this right now. I just don't know," was Rich's response.

We kept on walking, nailing signs to poles, letting the question hang in the air, knowing that sooner or later, we would have to answer it.

The streets were unnaturally quiet for a Saturday af-ternoon. Rich and I were each wearing sneakers, which made no sound as we moved along. "I wonder if any-one up this way has seen Huckie," Rich said to me. "I think we ought to try ringing a couple of doorbells and ask. Let's just start going to houses where it looks like people are home."

"No one is home," I said. "It feels like a ghost town."

"People must be home. There are a lot of cars in driveways," Rich observed. "Let's just pick a house."

I liked the idea. I was willing to drop my question about having an end point. I was desperate to hear someone, anyone, say something about Huck. I was not the least bit reluctant to stand on strangers' doorsteps and ask if they had any clue at all about Huck.

As we got to the end of Fawn Hill Drive, where it intersects with Deerfield Terrace, we saw a mustard yellow spilt-level house with brown trim. Wood was piled high in the side yard, covered by a black tarp. We were about to walk up the front steps when a middle-aged, somewhat large man, with an earnest look, came around from the back of the house. "Are you looking for a red dog?" he asked.

My heart began to race. I could not believe what I was hearing. I nearly started to cry. Rich was cautiously hopeful.

"Yes, yes, we are," he said quickly. He showed the man the flyer.

"You know, that's the dog. He sat right out there by the logs all morning long. In fact, when I told my wife about it, she said she saw a sign about a lost dog in the supermarket. She just now went back to the store to take down the phone number."

Rich and I were both trying to process what the

man was saying. "So you saw our dog this morning," Rich said. "How long ago was that?"

"Must be a couple of hours ago," the man replied. "I tried to get him, 'cause he looked lost. He looked like he belonged to somebody, but looked lost," the man continued. "I was out with my rottweiler, and when your dog saw me and saw my dog, he just took off. Darnedest thing, he took off like a jackrabbit. There was no getting him."

My heart sank. The pitch of emotion was overwhelming. I could not imagine how Huck was surviving, or what kind of physical shape he must be in by now. What sorts of harrowing experiences was he having, and how much longer could he possibly go on this way? On the morning he ran from the Clarks, he weighed barely nine pounds. How could he sustain himself?

But Rich was not sinking at all. Quite the opposite— his spirits were boosted by the fact that Huck had been seen alive after yet another cold night roaming the wild. He also knew now that Dave had made the right call. We had moved the publicity in the right direction.

Rich asked the man which way Huck had run, and the man pointed to Youngs Road, a narrow, winding, busy road where people drove their cars faster than they should. At that, Rich's own emotions, so optimistic a moment ago, took a dive. Sensing Rich's sudden change of mood, the man cautioned, "But, you know, I can't be sure."

"Thanks very much for your help," Rich said. "If you see him again, call any of those numbers."

"You bet I will," the man said.

We started walking toward the street. Rich called Dave on his cell phone to let him know what we had learned. Dave's response was much like Rich's, though without the noticeable mood swing.

"Well, the good part is that he was alive as of a few hours ago, which all by itself is pretty amazing," Dave said. "You know, in addition to everything else, it was cold last night."

"And what's the bad part?" Rich asked.

Without hesitating, Dave said, "That the guy wasn't able to catch him and that Huck ran toward Youngs."

The hour was getting late, the day was growing darker.

"I've got to head back to the house for a while to take care of a few things and to see about Darian," Dave said. "Michael and Ray will meet you at your car. I'll catch up with you later."

"Okay," Rich replied. "Thanks for everything this morning."

Rich and I continued putting up flyers. We must have posted Huck's picture on every tree and telephone pole in the neighborhood. In the process, we feverishly searched yards for our dog, calling to him as we did.

"HUCK, HUCK, HUCKIE. HUCK, COME ON, BOY."

But we heard no bark, saw no flash of red hair against the brown, dull terrain. Feeling miserable, we walked to our car. We had to regroup yet again, figure out our next steps, given that we now knew where Huck had been early that morning.

Michael ran down the street toward me. "Mom, what happened?" he asked excitedly. "Uncle Dave said someone saw Huck this morning."

I put my hand on Michael's cheek before telling him once again that Huck had been seen but had fled. "Someone did see Huck. He said Huck sat by a pile of wood next to his house all morning," I explained. "The man tried to get Huck, but Huck ran."

"How are we ever going to catch him?" Michael asked plaintively, his emotions raw.

Before I could answer, Rich did. He crouched down so he could look into Michael's eyes. "Listen, lovee, we know Huck is still alive, which is the most important thing of all," he said. "And we know we are on his trail, that we keep finding ourselves in places where he has been. Now if we had had food with us last night, we would have been able to get him," Rich continued. "That was my fault. I won't let that happen again. But let's keep in mind, Huck is alive."

Michael was trying to work it all out in his own head, trying to assure himself that somehow fate would allow the moment when Huck would be seen, we would be called, and we would all be reunited. He wanted to believe our story would have a happy ending.

As painful as it would have been, I would have preferred that Rich at least touch on the idea that despite our seeming proximity to him, Huck might disappear from our lives forever. But it wasn't in Rich's DNA to do that.

"But what about other people who see him and then he just runs away?" Michael continued. "How is that ever going to change?"

Rich remained steadfast in his optimism. "That's what the signs are for. If any one of the people who have seen Huck so far had seen our flyer beforehand and knew to offer Huck cream cheese, they probably would have been able to catch him."

He added: "And Michael, I know you have seen this for yourself, the people who live out here have been so generous to us, so open and kind. They want to help us. We have a lot of people looking for Huck, trying as hard as they can to help us."

All that may have been true, but it was also true that Huck was still out there, facing death at every turn—a speeding car or truck, a wild animal like a coyote or a bear, an aggressive bird of prey, starvation, dehydration. The woods were even deeper here than they were in the Carriage Lane area, and they covered much of the terrain. The sky was now getting much darker, a storm was brewing. It would be another threat to Huck's survival. It would also drive us indoors, forcing us to lose precious hours of daylight.

We had plastered the area with signs. Luck had led us to a man who had seen Huck, but the very same man reported that Huck had taken off yet again. There was no point in ringing any more doorbells on Fawn Hill Drive.

We got back in the car. Rich said he would drop Ray where he had locked his bike that morning so that he could get home now before it rained. About to pull the car away, Rich unwittingly put the car in reverse instead of drive, and backed into a lamppost, one with Huck's picture on it.

"Damn," he yelled. He put the car in park and got out to see if there had been any damage done to either the car or the lamppost. He seemed to be taking a long time, which led me to believe there had been damage, a complication we surely did not need. I was about to get out of the car, when Rich got back in. "It's okay. Sorry about that, guys," he said. And we drove back down to Carriage Lane and Ray's bike without saying very much.

When we got there, Ray offered to come out again later, after the rain. Rich was starting to feel self-conscious about taking up so much of Ray's free time. "You have been so nice and so helpful," Rich said to Ray. "But I don't want you to spend your entire day helping us."

"No, that's okay. I want to help," Ray said. "Really."

Ray's desire to be a constant member of the search party was touching. Here was a teenage boy giving up hours and hours of precious weekend time to comb the woods looking for a dog that belonged to people he had never met before. In many ways, Ray was the embodiment of the good cheer and open hearts we had encountered all over town the past few days.

"Why don't we talk later and see where things are by then?" Rich said.

"Great. I'll talk to you later," Ray responded. He got out of the car and we watched as he unlocked his bike, waved at us, and pedaled away.

Rich, Michael, and I sat in the car for a moment and started to talk about what we should do next. Rich started retelling the conversations he had earlier in the morning. He told us about Dick Seelbach and how Dick had watched Huck all afternoon on Friday, and about the bologna and cream cheese he let Rich leave on the edge of his driveway. Rich went over the story of Brian O'Callahan and how Brian had heard Huck late at night in his yard.

"I think we should give everyone on that street a flyer," Michael proposed. "We could put them in their mailboxes or through the handles of their doors."

It was a good idea, given that two people on that street had seen or heard Huck. Still, the information was a day old, and Huck clearly was no longer around there. He had been seen that morning in a place at least à mile north.

Rich was thinking about Michael's suggestion but also thinking ahead to what made sense next. "Do you know if the Clarks have gotten any calls today?" Rich asked me.

"I doubt it," I said. "I think Barbara would have called to let me know."

"Why don't you call her, just in case?" he said.

Before I had a chance to dial Barbara's number, she called me. "Listen, Darian just got home from practice. I think you should bring Michael over here for a while to give him a little break and let him have some lunch," she suggested.

"I don't know if he'll go, but I'll ask him," I said. "We're just trying to figure out what's next. Have you gotten any calls so far today?" I asked.

"Not a one. I'm really kind of surprised," Barbara said. "Maybe it is just that people have been out. Maybe we'll hear something later."

"Let me call you back once we plan our next move," I said.

Michael had overheard enough of the conversation to surmise that Barbara was urging he have some downtime. "I want to stay with Dad," he said. "I don't want to go back to the Clarks."

I told Rich and Michael the distressing news that

there had not been a single call all day. Other than the man with the tarp-covered pile of wood, as far as we knew, no one else had seen Huck all morning or into the afternoon. There was only one more X to put on Dave's tracking map.

Thinking that we may have left the area where Huck had been seen that morning prematurely, I suggested we go back up the streets around Fawn Hill Drive, or else that we put up signs on trees and poles in Ramsey. It was impossible to know what to do and I was easily pulled away from my own ideas, something completely out of character for me.

Michael was not so easily swayed. At that moment he was insistent about staying on Carriage Lane, in the neighborhood where the night before he had come so close to holding Huck in his arms again. He thought Huck would return there. He wanted to go to the Seelbach house to see if the bologna and cream cheese had magically lured Huck back to the area.

I don't think either Rich or I wanted to tell Michael that we thought his notion was the least likely of scenarios. "How about this?" Rich proposed. "Michael, you and I will drop Mom back on Main Street, and she can start nailing up the posters to trees and poles there. Then we'll come back here and look some more. We'll do what you said and make sure everyone on the block has a copy of the flyer. Then we'll meet Mom back at the Clarks' house and have something to eat before going back up to Fawn Hill Drive."

Michael was satisfied. He had been heard. "That sounds like a good idea," he said.

I knew it was more than likely a waste of time, though I did think both Michael and I were being guided by wanting to return to where Huck had been. For Michael, it was a matter of returning to where he had seen Huck with his own eyes. For me, it was a matter of returning to the place where anyone had last laid eyes on Huck.

As I called Barbara back and told her our plan, Rich started driving back toward Main Street. Just as they had done the day before, Rich and Michael dropped me at the top, past the high school, only this time I was carrying a hammer and nails, along with posters covered in plastic. I suddenly realized that I did not even know if what I was doing, or, for that matter, what we had all been doing all morning, was legal. I hadn't given it a thought before now. I imagined myself standing in front of a judge explaining to him why I had defaced every telephone pole in Ramsey and Mahwah. In my fantasy, he was lenient, since he had his own dog and son.

I I I

Rich and Michael headed once more to Pine Tree Road. Michael was heartened now that the adults or at least one of them was following his lead. "I want to go back into the woods where we saw Huck run last night," Michael said. "I just think he might be there."

Michael had a desperate need to search those woods for himself. Ever since he had watched Huck run into the thicket of trees and brush, Michael could not understand why his beloved dog would run from him and not to him. Wasn't the sound of his voice enough to bring Huck home? Didn't Huck ache for Michael as much as Michael ached for Huck?

When Michael and Rich got out of the car on Pine Tree Road, Michael got down on his hands and knees in front of the car to try and understand what the car must have looked like from Huck's perspective, to try and gain some understanding of why Huck had run.

"If you are a little puppy, the car looks pretty scary from down here," Michael said to Rich. "All you can really see are these blinding lights and this big machine that looks like it could squash you in a second. You can't even see the windshield from down here to see people's faces," Michael described while still on his knees in front of the parked car.

"I'll bet with the car running, he didn't even hear me call to him. He just ran because he was afraid of the car."

"I'll bet you are right," Rich said, reaching down to give Michael a hand up.

Rich and Michael first walked up one side of the

street and then down the other, leaving a flyer in every curbside mailbox or stuffed between the storm door and front door of every house. Then they did the same on nearby Carriage Lane, before going into the woods for one more look. They saw the bologna and the cream cheese untouched in front of the Seelbach house. Unbeknownst to Michael, Rich was determined to make quick work of this latest search of the woods. He was doing it only to satisfy his son. Just as I was, Rich was eager to get back up to Fawn Hill Drive.

Rich and Michael traipsed through the grove of bare trees. As they moved toward the edge, near Carriage Lane, they spotted a father and his two young sons, out with a spirited dog, a Shiba Inu, about four times the size of Huck. "Let's talk to them," Rich said to Michael.

When they were closer to the family, the man called out. "Are you looking for something?" the father asked Rich. He walked toward Rich, stuck out his hand, and said, "Hi, I'm Ben Mamola. And these are my sons, Ben and Peter, and that's our dog, Scooter. We live right here," he added and pointed to a sprawling house up against the edge of the woods.

Ben was in his thirties, a vigorous, handsome man, with dark hair, and dark eyes, who was unusually open and friendly, even for Ramsey. "We saw you in the woods and it looked like you were looking for something, rather than just out for a walk, so we thought we'd ask."

Rich introduced himself and Michael and started explaining what, or rather who, they were looking for, and how they happened to end up in the woods bordering the side yard of the Mamola home. Ben seemed to be listening intently to Rich's every word. It made Rich, who had long tired of repeating our tale, want to tell Ben every detail—all about the cancer, and getting Huck, and going away on vacation, and losing Huck. He told him about our close call of last night.

Rich's unfailing devotion to his family, his ardent and relentless search for the family dog, touched Ben deeply. Ben could feel Rich's anguish. Madly in love with his own wife, Ben kept mulling over what it must have felt like for Rich to have had a sick wife, to have taken her away to celebrate good health, and then to have had the celebration fall apart.

Then Ben's older son, Ben Jr., a boy of about five or six, volunteered the family: "Dad, let's help them look for their dog."

"We're going to," Ben replied. "This is the oddest thing," he said to Rich, "but it feels like I've known you all my life. Let me help. We know these woods really well. Why don't you let us look here, and then we'll get in the car and head up toward Mahwah."

Even though so many people in Ramsey had gone above and beyond the niceties, had been far more than merely polite or courteous, had truly befriended us outsiders, Ben's offer of turning over his Saturday afternoon to help us look for Huck still struck Rich as extraordinary.

In a twist on the character played by Jack Lemmon in the movie *The Out-of-Towners*, an abrasive man who had kept a log of names and phone numbers of people who had wronged him and his exasperated wife on their trip from Twin Oaks, Ohio, to New York, Rich was keeping a log of all the names and phone numbers of people who had helped us, with the intention of thanking them when our saga ended. No matter how it ended. The list was long. Now it included Ben Mamola.

"That would be a huge help," Rich said in response to Ben's offer. "But are you sure? I'd hate for you to lose the better part of Saturday afternoon."

"Not a problem at all," Ben said. "My wife is away on a church retreat. The boys and I were going to do some errands this afternoon, but the errands can wait."

"You are a great guy. Thank you so much," Rich said as he put his arm on Ben's back in a gesture of warmth and gratitude. "Let me give you a copy of our flyer, which will give you a picture of Huck and also all of our contact numbers."

Ben and his wife, Catherine, were active participants at St. Paul's, Ramsey's Catholic church. Catherine was spending the weekend at a women's church retreat called "Cornerstone," at which the participants give testimony and talk in depth with each other about their own singular life-changing events. For some of the women, coming to terms was painful; for others, it was a chance to give thanks.

Ben had met Catherine on a blind date of sorts on a warm night in May of 1993, at a bar in Clifton, New Jersey, called Yakety Yaks. "I took one look at her and thought, this won't work, there's got to be something wrong, she's too beautiful," Ben said, as he recalled the first moment he laid eyes on the pretty, blond Catherine.

But it did work. He introduced her to his parents over the July 4th weekend, and they were engaged by October and married the following August. The two of them succeeded at one career after another. She, having given up a Manhattan-centered career in marketing to stay home with their children, then took up oil painting and established herself as an artist, selling her works through a gallery in Rhode Island. And he, giving up Wall Street for private investing, then gave that up because he wanted to feel that he was actually making something. He had been trained as a chemical engineer, and after meeting someone at church who sparked an idea about using omega-3 in consumer products, he started Zymes, a company on a mission to do just that.

Rich was grateful to Ben, for his undaunted spirit, and the selfless way he made himself and his sons available to help us do the impossible—find our small dog in the warren of streets and woods.

Ben also made an impression on Michael. "Wow. I can't believe how nice that guy was," Michael said to Rich as they walked back to Pine Tree to get the car. "He said he's not just going to look in the woods by his house, but go to Mahwah, too. That is unbelievable."

| | |

The rain, which had been threatening all day with periodic drizzle, was now turning into a steady shower. I had put up flyers inside their plastic covers all the way down Ramsey's Main Street and onto Wyckoff Avenue until I ran out of them. My hands were sore from driving the nails into poles and trees. I made it back to the Clarks' house just before the rain teemed down. Rich and Michael came through the back door and into the kitchen shortly after me.

Barbara and Dave were sitting at the kitchen table staring down at the map with Dave's markings. "Do we have anything new to add?" Dave asked.

"No," Rich and I said at the same time.

"I met a guy who saw him all afternoon on Friday, before we did," Rich started to explain. "And then that other guy I told you about who heard him in the yard last night. And we just met another guy in the same neighborhood who said he was going to take his sons and look in those woods back on Pine Tree and then take a ride up in the Mahwah area where Huck was this morning," Rich said. "But no, we have no new sightings."

"Yeah, but the guy who saw Huck on Friday afternoon is a new sighting," Dave said. "It is not recent and it is the same area where we know he was on Friday evening, but still, it is another sighting, another point on the map."

"That's true," Rich said. "Let's look at the map and see if we can figure out whether or not it makes sense for us to go back up to Fawn Hill Drive." While we all stood poring over the map watching Dave trace Huck's movements, or at least what we knew of Huck's movements from the reports we had, Michael went upstairs to find Darian.

Assuming their war general pose over the map, Rich and Dave were at a loss. "It is hard to know, but I think it makes the most sense right now for us to go back to the streets surrounding Fawn Hill Drive," Rich said. "That is the last place he was seen alive, and we don't have any other sightings that would suggest he's moved out of that area."

The lousy weather was not a deterrent for me and I knew it would not be for Rich. But I didn't want Michael out, walking around in the freezing cold rain. I thought it best if Rich and I went alone. The challenge would be convincing Michael.

"Just go," Barbara said. "Michael's upstairs with Darian. I'll let him know you went."

"I can't do that," I said. "I have to tell him we are going." I did not have to look at Barbara to know she was rolling her eyes.

To my surprise, when I broached the subject with Michael, he was amenable to staying behind. What he was not amenable to, though, was having lunch. Over the past few days, he had eaten some, but very little, certainly not enough for a growing boy. I was constantly worried about it.

I I I

Rich and I borrowed a couple of umbrellas from Barbara, got in the car, and drove back to Fawn Hill Drive and the neighborhoods of Mahwah, the town that encircles Ramsey. On our way, we passed many of the signs we had put up that morning, all of which were holding up well despite the weather, thanks to Rich's foresight and the plastic sleeves.

We started out by the house where Huck had last been seen, by the piles of wood covered with tarp. It was still raining. Traveling now on foot, we searched that street and the ones nearby. We explored every yard and every tree-filled empty lot, desperately looking for Huck. We rang doorbells and stopped cars. We looked behind garages, around garbage cans, under slides and swings, inside open shed doors, underneath anything that might provide a small frightened animal shelter from the elements. As we trudged through the mud and stepped ankle deep into puddles, we called to Huck again and again, our voices begging him to come out from wherever he might be. Minutes turned into hours, and the afternoon turned into early evening. Darkness was falling.

By the time we decided to get back in the car, I was hoarse. I sat next to Rich in the front seat looking at how thoroughly drenched he was. I could see even now that his mind was racing, trying to figure out what else we could do in the waning minutes of daylight. I knew he could not stop. I, though, drenched and distraught, was again wondering how much longer we could all go on this way. And then I pictured Huck, cold and soaked through, somewhere, and wondered how much longer *he* could go on.

We agreed to drive around some, to use what precious little daylight was left to keep our eyes trained on the landscape. It was no use. We both knew it was no use. After the man saw Huck by that woodpile this morning, Huck seemed to have vanished. We had put up all of our signs and no one had called. The trail had gone stone cold.

For a moment, Rich broke the silence. "Huck could

be miles away from here, or we could be passing him right now and not even know it."

I didn't want to add what we both had considered. Huck might be dead. We drove back to the Clarks.

Barbara and Dave knew. They knew we would come home soaked to the bone and without hope. They did what they knew to do. They had a fire blazing in the fireplace, and Dave offered Rich a stiff drink, even though he knew Rich was not ready to let go.

They reported that no calls had come in all day long. Michael and Darian came downstairs and joined all of us in the kitchen. Michael did not ask about our latest search. He just moved close to me and leaned his body into my lap without really sitting there, the way children that age often do.

Barbara was moving between the sink and the refrigerator, sometimes for no reason at all. The rest of us were staring at the map, still spread out on the kitchen table, as though it would hold the answer to Huck's whereabouts, to whether he was still alive, and to where we would see him if only we would look.

Eventually, Dave folded the map and Barbara set the table for dinner. They had ordered a few pizzas and some salad from a local restaurant. None of us ate very much. After dinner, Rich and I sat by the fire. Barbara and Dave loaded the dishes into the dishwasher and then joined us in front of the fire. Michael and Darian went upstairs to watch the TV in Barbara and Dave's bedroom.

The phone did not, would not ring.

Michael fell asleep on the floor in front of the TV and after he had been asleep for a time, I woke him and told him we had to head back to the hotel. We said good night to the Clarks and once again headed back to the Woodcliff Lake Hilton. All of the stores on Ramsey's Main Street were closed and locked tight, just as they had been when Rich had set out early that morning.

"I don't want to go back to the hotel," Michael said sleepily as we pulled into the hotel parking lot. "I want to keep looking for Huck."

It was heartbreaking. Somehow Rich found it in himself to assure Michael that we would be back at it tomorrow, that Huck had proven he could get through two nights, and that he would again. I don't know where Rich was getting the emotional strength for this. I was empty.

Rich offered to let Michael and me off in front of the hotel so we would not have to walk through the parking lot in the rain. It was absolutely pouring. But we declined, and we all parked the car together and walked in the rain together into the hotel and across the lobby's marble floor to the elevator and up to our room.

We each needed a shower. Michael went first, taking what was a specialty of his, a twenty-second shower. I settled him in bed. He was asleep instantly. I took a quick shower, too, though longer than twenty seconds.

Rich plugged in his cell phone to recharge the constantly draining battery. Without thinking much about it, he turned the phone off. He was the last one in the shower, and he, too, was quick. I got into bed. When Rich came out of the bathroom, he slid in alongside me, and turned out the light.

Depressed, my body aching, I closed my eyes, listening to the rain and the howling wind. I thought we ought to call the search off. I tried to imagine how I would tell Michael that these things happen in life and that we had tried as hard as we could to find Huck but that Huck was gone. I would tell him how sorry I was, how I knew how much it hurt, how I would be there to help him get through it. As painful as that would be for us both, I thought it was the right thing to do. I thought I'd be protecting him from this constant, day-in and day-out emotional upheaval we were in. I thought the time had come to help Michael come to terms with his devastating loss.

Rich, too, had closed his eyes. But his thoughts could not have been more different. He was thinking about how long he could keep this going. He thought we'd stay in the hotel for a while longer and keep looking, keep running ads in the paper, keep putting up flyers, and talking to people as they went to work or brought their garbage cans to the road. We'd pay for radio ads. Rich had figured out that once I had to go back to work and Michael to school, he could continue to come out to New Jersey by himself whenever he could afford to take the time from his work. He thought we could afford to drain our savings of thousands more dollars. He had decided to search for another six weeks. Only then, he thought, could he really face Michael and tell him we had done everything we possibly could.

Rich's last thought that night was of Huck and the cold rain hitting the window of our hotel room. He knew Huck could make it through another night, could elude becoming the prey of wild animals, but he did not know how much more difficult survival would be with the addition of the driving rain. Rich fell asleep praying Huck was still alive.

CHAPTER 14

A T 6:30 SUNDAY MORNING, the hotel phone rang in our room, startling all of us out of sleep. I was disoriented for a few seconds, but managed enough coherence to wonder who could possibly be calling so early on the hotel phone, especially since the signs all had Rich's cell-phone number and so did the Clarks. I picked up the receiver and nearly inaudibly said, "Hello."

"Why isn't anyone answering Rich's cell phone?" Barbara shrieked at me. "Get up. We had a call; a man saw Huck just a few minutes ago. You have to hurry. Get to Fawn Hill and Youngs."

Before I really grasped what she was saying, and certainly before I told Rich where we were to go, I screamed at Rich and Michael, "Get dressed. Hurry up. Someone has just seen Huck. We have to move fast."

"Janet, Janet," Barbara called, trying to get me to reengage in our phone call. "Dave has already left. Does Rich know how to get to the intersection of Fawn Hill and Youngs?"

I called to Rich, "Do you know how to get to Fawn Hill and Youngs?"

And without waiting for an answer, before Rich had a chance to get his socks on, I thrust the phone toward him and said: "Why don't you get the information from Barbara?"

Michael was in the bathroom and caught a glimpse of himself in the mirror. He stood there for a second and thought, *I'll bet this is it. We might really find Huck right now. This has to be it. I can't lose him again.* He allowed himself a smile before he walked out of the bathroom.

Rich was now off the phone with Barbara, tying his sneakers as fast as he could. "Damn it. I can't believe I turned off that cell phone. What was I thinking?" he said into the air. "Barbara had to lose minutes finding the number of the hotel."

"Forget about it," I said. "Let's go."

We were all in various stages of dress and no one had a jacket on. Rich grabbed the bologna and the cream cheese. "Take jackets," I yelled.

And with that, we were out the door. Michael was the last one out, reaching for his lucky green Yankees cap as he left the room. We ran down the hall. Anxiously, I pushed the elevator button again and again and again before it came. The three of us ran through the lobby toward the front door. The hotel manager called to us: "Stop. Slow down. Don't run in the lobby. It is not allowed."

We completely ignored him. We flew through the lobby and then the puddle-filled parking lot and into the car. Michael was in the backseat. Rich handed him the bologna and the cream cheese.

I have no idea how fast Rich was going, but I am certain he was speeding, past Elmer's, down Main Street in Ramsey, and up to Fawn Hill Drive, the area where Rich and I had been late Saturday afternoon. At some point Rich looked in his rearview mirror to look at Michael and saw him eating a piece of bologna.

"I'm glad to see you eating, lovee, but you'd better save that for Huck."

"Oh yeah," Michael said with a grin on his face. He stuffed what was left in the package into the pocket of his jacket along with the cream cheese.

Dave was already there, having parked his car on the Fawn Hill side of the intersection. Rich parked our car on the Youngs Road side. We stood on Fawn Hill Drive looking at the first house on that street. It was a ranch house, with gray-blue shutters. It had a deep, sloping front yard. But it wasn't clear whether that was the house at the intersection or whether it was the white-shingled house at the end of Youngs Road.

"I don't know which house the guy who called meant when he said he saw him at the intersection," Dave said. "Huck is obviously not out front, so why don't we look around the back."

Rich and Dave were once again strategizing. "It looks like the yards run into each other. Why don't you and Michael go around that side," Rich said pointing to the far side of that first house on Fawn Hill. "Janet and I will approach it from Youngs."

As relieved and astounded as I was that Huck had made it through another night, a fiercely stormy night, I didn't want to mention that I thought Huck was gone again. The man who called in the tip said Huck was at the intersection. Well, he wasn't at the intersection. In fact, he wasn't anyplace nearby that you could see from the car. We missed him. A fair amount of time must have passed between when the man who saw him called Barbara, Barbara called us, and we got there. For whatever reason, we just didn't get there fast enough.

The houses in this area were all set up on a hill. Rich and I climbed the hill, which was slippery because the grass was wet from the downpour the night before. Even though the sun was breaking through, it was still too early for the ground to have dried. Rich reached the top of the hill first and turned to see how far I was lagging. As soon as I reached the top, we walked into the yard behind the house.

Rich started quietly saying something, over and over, something he would say to Huck at times when they would play around on the living room floor: "Are you a good boy? Yes you are a good boy." It was one of those nonsensical, rhythmic things people suddenly find themselves saying to pets. It was a term of endearment. Rich was hoping Huck would hear it and come back to us.

Startled, I grabbed Rich's arm to keep myself from screaming. There, just standing there, was Huck. He was about twenty-five feet away.

Huck looked weary and his hair was matted. He looked at Rich, who then started to get down on his knees, but before he did, Huck turned and trotted away. Huck didn't run, which made me wonder if he was injured. We were about to follow, when Rich's cell phone rang.

It was Dave calling from the other side of the house. "Michael sees Huck," he said. "Huck is about thirty feet away from him."

The moment Michael saw Huck, he summoned all of his self-control. He did not make any quick movements. He squatted. Then he gingerly reached into his jacket pocket and pulled out a piece of bologna. He put it on the ground in front of him. He ever so slowly put his hand back in his pocket and managed to open the tub of cream cheese enough to stick his finger into it, intending to rub the cream cheese on the bologna. Michael had managed to go from squatting to kneeling without making a sound.

"Huck is now about twenty-five feet away," Dave whispered into the phone.

Rich and I behind the house on one side of the yard, and Dave, out of our line of sight, on the other side, each stood frozen in place.

"Hi Huck, how are you, boy?" Michael said softly. "I've missed you. Are you hungry? Do you want some cream cheese?"

"He is now about twenty feet away," Dave whispered into the phone. "Now he's about fifteen feet away."

"Hi, Huckie boy." Michael kept his soft-spoken entreaty to Huck going. "You want some cream cheese?"

It was all Michael could do to hold himself together. He wanted to swoop Huck up in his arms and cry and laugh with abandon. But he was as controlled as a major-league player about to make the winning play in the last at bat of a World Series game.

Rich, with the phone pressed to his ear, stood somewhat bent so that I could have my head right up against his, even though I could not hear a thing.

Dave whispered into the phone, "Huck is now ten feet away from Michael."

"Huck is ten feet away from Michael," Rich repeated to me, as he did after every report from Dave.

"He's about eight feet away."

"He's about six feet away."

"Huck is about four feet away."

Huck took another step toward Michael and when Michael reached for him, Huck took several steps backward. Michael feared he would run.

"Huck just backed away," Dave said.

It was an eternity before Rich and I heard another update over the phone from Dave.

"We thought he'd run, but he didn't. Now I'd say Huck is about five feet away."

"Huck is about four feet away."

"He's three feet away."

"He's two feet away."

"Michael has Huck in his arms."

Rich and I went tearing around to the other side of the yard. Michael was hugging his dog, his best friend, his most trusted confidante, the pet he had longed for his entire young life, the antidote to his mother's brush with death. "I love you, Huck. I missed you so much. Where have you been, boy?" he said sweetly.

Huck, licking Michael's face, his lips, his cheeks, his nose, even his eyes, was too busy to answer.

Dave, who was filled with emotion, spoke in a louder voice than Michael had ever heard him, "Let's get him in the car and close all the windows." He was fearful Huck would bolt again.

At the sight of our son and his dog in the backseat of Dave's car, finally reunited, with Michael smiling and laughing and Huck licking him and climbing all over Michael's head, Rich and I were each overcome with tears of joy.

A woman, still in her bathrobe, came out of her house and stood on her front steps for a minute looking at Rich, who was jumping up and down and punching the air with his fists. "Did you find your dog?" she called to us.

"Yes, yes, we did," I called back to her, laughing at Rich's antics.

"We sure did," Rich shouted. "Thanks for asking."

"Congratulations," the woman said, smiling.

Rich pulled something out of his pocket I didn't know was there—Huck's leash. When we were standing by Dave's car, Rich knocked on the window of the backseat and told Michael to crack the window. He fed the leash through the window. As he did, Huck started licking the window. Rich told Michael to put the leash on Huck and wrap the other end of it around his hand. We were not taking any chances.

Once Michael attached the leash and was holding the end of it securely, I carefully opened the other door to the backseat and got in. I was again overcome with emotion. With Huck jumping on us both, I hugged Michael. I then held Huck in my arms and kissed him before he licked my face. I handed him back to Michael. I was about to get out of the car when Dave got in and said, "Rich said you should stay in my car and we'll meet him back at the house."

I felt badly that Rich, the field general, the optimist in chief, the tireless father and husband, had not yet had a chance to hold our newly found Huck. If not for his insistence that this could be done, that we could somehow find our puppy in the dense woods in the foothills of the mountains, the overwhelming joy of the moment would not have been ours.

Chapter 15

RICH GOT BACK to the Clarks' house before we did and was waiting for us on the driveway. He motioned to Michael to stay in the car for a moment. Once Dave, Rich, and I had formed a phalanx next to the car door, Rich opened Michael's door so Michael could get out while still holding Huck in his arms and keeping the leash tightly wound around his hand.

Like Secret Service agents protecting a presidential candidate, we moved as a unit up the stone path and through the front door. In retrospect, it was a hilarious moment, but at the time, it seemed right.

"Don't put him down until we are sure the back door is closed," Dave said.

Barbara was in the kitchen making coffee. She came running toward the living room. The usually calm, take-life-as-it-comes Dave sent her back. "Make sure the back door is closed," he said to her. "Lock it."

Barbara dashed back into the kitchen and then ran toward Michael and Huck. "Oh my God," she said, tears running down her face. "Darian, come down here. Quick!" she called.

Darian ran down the stairs in her pajamas and bare feet taking the steps two and three at a time. "Huck," she yelled with glee at her first sight of him. "How did you find him?"

Without waiting for an answer, she started petting Huck's head and kissing him. Barbara could not let go of Michael who could not let go of Huck. Dave, satisfied the house was locked up, said to Michael: "You can put him down now."

But Michael didn't. He turned and handed him to Rich. And for the third time that morning, I felt my eyes fill with tears.

"Hiya, boy," Rich said, taking Huck into his arms. Huck could not get enough of Rich, who was laughing. The laughter grew louder with every lick Huck planted on Rich's face. Huck looked journey worn but seemed to be his sweet, open self.

Rich handed Huck back to Michael, who carried him into the kitchen with all of us following behind. The anguish of the past few days had been replaced by pure happiness.

We were all wondering who the man was who had called so early in the morning to alert us to Huck's whereabouts. He had appeared like the angel, Clarence Oddbody, in the Christmas movie *It's a Wonderful Life*, who materializes in George Bailey's life at a moment of utter despair.

"Barbara has his number," Dave said. "His name is John something, and he lives right around where we found Huck."

John turned out to be seventy-three-year-old John Mantineo, a tall, humble man with white hair and blue eyes, the husband of Janet, and the father of six children, all grown and out of the house except for his twenty-seven-year-old son, Michael, who has Down syndrome. Many of John and Janet's children are in helping professions and are married to people in helping professions—firefighters, police officers, teachers, nurses, emergency room technicians. Their photographs line the bedroom hallway and cover the white refrigerator in the family's split-level yellow house on Deerfield Terrace, just off Fawn Hill Drive.

Among the photographs is a framed reprint of a newspaper article about his Michael, who at the age of thirteen, as part of a 4-H project, spent endless hours taking his own pets—cats, dogs, rabbits, and guinea pigs—to visit elderly people in nearby nursing homes. Michael has a way with animals. He's won ribbons at dog shows and trophies for horseback riding in the Special Olympics.

As a small child Michael had many pets. By the time he was in his twenties, he was working in the Franklin Lakes Animal Hospital.

John and Janet raised their remarkable family on John's salary as a field engineer for the Bergen County Parks Department where he went to work after he got out of the army in 1955. After he retired, he delivered flowers and did some carpentry work.

Late in the day on Saturday, John had seen one of our flyers nailed to a telephone pole. He thought surely a dog that small would be nabbed by a wild animal. Just recently, Janet had thrown rocks at a crow to get the crow to drop from its beak the baby rabbit it had plucked right out of its mother's nest. John knew there were not only birds of prey in the area but coyotes and foxes and bears. He had gone home to get a pen and a piece of paper and had come back to the sign to write down the number.

The next morning, John did what he always did on Sunday mornings before the family went to church. At the crack of dawn, he got up for the seven-mile drive to Bagel Train in Suffern to buy bagels, remembering to include sesame bagels and everything bagels in his bagful.

On this Sunday morning, his trip to the bagel store was interrupted when he saw a bedraggled, red-haired puppy sitting at the intersection. Certain it was the dog pictured on the flyer, he got out of his tan Malibu and called "cream cheese." But the dog ran from him. John went home and called the number, waking Barbara and Dave.

Later that morning, the Mantineos went to Mass at Immaculate Conception Church in Mahwah, where John and Janet volunteer as greeters and Michael is an altar server. "I like to be close to God," Michael says of the experience. The next time they heard anything at all about the dog, it was that the dog had been found, thanks to John's call.

In the Clarks' kitchen that morning, there was nothing but smiles and jockeying to get close to Huck. I wanted to get Huck something to eat, and somehow his dog food did not seem like the right thing. "Barbara, do you have any yogurt?" I asked, knowing it was something Huck loved and thinking it might be something he could easily handle.

"I don't," she said.

Dave and I decided we would go out and get yogurt for Huck and bagels for everyone else.

Rich was already thinking ahead, reminding me we had to check out of the hotel and take down as many of the flyers as we could. Then his cell phone rang. It was Ray, who was up, ready to spend the day with us searching for Huck.

"We found him!" Rich said triumphantly.

"You found him? How? Where? Can I see him?" Ray asked all at once. "Where are you now?"

"We're still at my sister-in-law's," Rich said. "Why don't you come over here and have bagels with us?"

By the time Dave and I came back with the yogurt and the bagels, Ray had arrived and was sitting in the kitchen with everyone else, Huck still in Michael's arms. Ray stood and shook Rich's hand. "He's the best-looking poodle I have ever seen," Ray said, smiling broadly.

I handed Michael a container of cherry yogurt and a spoon. He stirred the yogurt, but before he could put a small amount on the spoon and tempt Huck, Huck had already put his snout in the container, practically inhaling the creamy treat. He licked the plastic container clean, the telltale signs all over his face.

When Michael finally put Huck down on the floor, Rich and I each noticed that Huck's right eye was more closed than his left eye. "We really should get Huck to the vet," I said. "It is possible we could get an appointment for today. I think Dr. Miller is sometimes there on Sundays."

I called.

"As long as there is no emergency, you can wait and bring him in tomorrow," said the young woman at the other end of the phone. "Is this about Huck?" she asked.

"Yes, yes, it is," I said, surprised that she knew Huck's name.

"You mean you found him?"

"Yes, we did."

"That's amazing!" she screamed. "Wait 'til I tell everyone. We were all worried. Everyone will be so happy. Dr. Miller will be here at eight thirty tomorrow morning. Can you bring him in then?"

"Sure," I said, relieved to have been given the first appointment of the day and touched that the office staff was so concerned.

We ate our bagels and watched Huck play on the floor, as though the harrowing adventure of the last few days had not even happened. But it did happen. And it had a happy ending. We learned a lot about the heart of a small town and the extraordinary level of concern one stranger can show another. We learned a lot about ourselves, too, about tenacity and grit and our devotion to one another.

Our remarkable journey had brought countless kind and generous people into our lives. We had to start to say thank you. Rich took a napkin and started to pen a letter to the editor of the free local paper, the *Town Journal*, thanking the townspeople of Ramsey, Mahwah, Allendale, and Wyckoff.

To the Editor:

On March 22, my wife, son, and I left New York for a ten-day vacation following a year of coping with serious health matters. We left our dog, Huckleberry, a toy red poodle puppy we bought for our son in part to help with our coping, with my wife's sister in Ramsey. One day into vacation we received a call that Huck ran away. We flew home and began a daybreak-to-darkness search. The generosity of the people of Ramsey, Mahwah, Wyckoff, and Allendale in terms of concern, prayer, and genuine assistance (people even changed plans to join in the search) was a life-changing experience. We believe in the basic goodness of people, but the people of those communities displayed deep empathy, even though it meant putting their own emotions on the line. Thanks to a tip, we found Huck seventy-two hours later. Along the way we found some terrific people, several of whom are now friends. We want to thank the people of those communities. We are deeply grateful for what you did.

Richard Pinsky
New York City

"I think this is it," Rich said, handing me the napkin. "I think it says what we want to say."

For once, I did not have anything to add or change, which is not always the case when one of us shows the other something one of us has written. Rich had said it all perfectly.

I was eager to go home. I wanted to take care of what we still needed to do in New Jersey, and then I wanted to get back to our lives. Rich and I were both nervous about leaving Michael and Huck behind and out of our sight while we went to check out of the hotel. We were worried someone would leave the back door open or that Huck would slip out of the Clarks' house in some other never-thought-of way. But we also knew we had a lot to do before we could pack our small family into the car and head back across the George Washington Bridge. And we knew that Barbara and Dave would be paying close attention to Huck's every move.

So we made quick work of checking out of the hotel. It was easy to pack, since we had never really unpacked. I paid the bill, while Rich got the car and loaded the suitcases into the trunk. He slammed it shut. "We are out of here," he said gleefully.

We drove past Elmer's and back into Ramsey. We parked about halfway down Main Street and tore down one sign after another. It seemed like everyone who spotted us pulling a sign off a pole or out of a shop window knew our tale. Some would ask about Huck by name. "Did you find Huck?" or "Did you find your dog?" A couple of women hugged me at hearing the news. Others shook our hands, while others just shouted, "Great news," or "Congratulations," as they got in their cars and drove away.

Some of the signs, like those in the schools or stores that were closed, would have to stay up until Monday, and we started making a list of people we knew we would have to call about them. We then headed for Pine Tree Road. We left a note for Brian O'Callahan, one of the men who had volunteered to look for Huck with his children, and another note for Dick Seelbach, the man who let us leave bologna on his driveway.

We went to Carriage Lane, where we found Ben Mamola and his wife, Catherine, who had just returned from her church retreat, taking bags out of the back of one of their cars. When we told them we had found Huck, there was a lot of hugging. We had just met Catherine, but she already knew our story well from Ben. "We've all been praying," Catherine said.

"Even the boys, before they went to bed last night, prayed you'd find your dog," Ben added. "Wait 'til they hear the news."

We thanked Ben for all his help and agreed to stay in touch. "You know," he said, "I believe everything happens for a reason."

Rich and I got back in the car and went back to the Clarks to pick up our son and our dog and head home. Michael did not ask to stay this time. He, too, was eager to be home.

Dave carried all of Huck's belongings, his bed, his toys, his food, out to the car and put them in the trunk. Michael carried Huck. We all lingered by the car, not really knowing what to say to one another. We hugged and laughed and lingered some more. The painful experience had deepened our love and respect for one another.

I got into the passenger side of the front seat. Michael handed Huck to me and waited for him to settle on my lap before he got in the backseat. Rich closed my door, then Michael's, and then got behind the wheel, put on his seat belt, and started the car. He looked at me and then at Michael, and asked, "Is this family ready to go home?"

"Let's go," Michael shouted happily from the backseat. The Clarks stood on their driveway waving as Rich backed the car out to the street.

I turned to look at a smiling Michael, sitting on the backseat, the lucky green Yankees cap on his head, tossing the 9/11 baseball Dave had given him into the air, the one that was supposed to inspire hope.

Afterword

HUCK RETURNED TO NEW YORK and to a very busy life. He became the hero of a bestselling book and the source of inspiration for people all over the world. Huck's tale, my family's tale, is a story about tenacity and hope. It is about hanging on against the odds in life, a choice most of us have to make in one way or another, whether we want to or not.

When we were desperately searching for Huck in the foothills of the Ramapo Mountains, it was impossible to imagine that not only would our story have a happy ending but that our experience would be an inspiration to others. Our simple story of faith, family devotion, and heroism has resonated with people facing their own personal trials.

I've received scores of letters and e-mails from people all over the world who have found meaning in

Huck's pages. There was Evan, a man in Australia facing his fourth cancer surgery, who said reading *Huck* had made him happy. Then there was Charlie, a middle-aged man from Minnesota, who said that though he's not a big reader, he did happen to read *Huck* and that as a result he started to see heroism in the lives of all kinds of people in his small community. And there was Max, the twelve-year-old boy who wrote to say he "LOVES THAT BOOK," and is thinking of naming his cat Huck. And, finally, there is Jill, a woman in Ohio, herself a cancer survivor who read *Huck* at the same time her daughter, Sasha, was undergoing chemotherapy. Jill wrote to me: "I shut down a long time ago, giving up on the basic goodness and generosity of people. I thought life was dark, something to be endured. But *Huck* has restored my faith."

Huck, the book, has been in many ways like Huck, the dog. Good things have come in its wake. New friendships have been forged. And I have reunited with old friends who, because of the vicissitudes of life, I had sadly lost touch with over the years. Two of them were at different times my "best" friend. Betsey Weldon, now Betsey Harabedian, was my next-door neighbor and best friend back in the Connecticut days. Until now, she was a memory, an eight-year-old standing next to me in a faded photograph taken on the day of our first Communion. And then there is Melanie O'Dea, my dearest pal throughout the tumultuous days of my teen years. It was no surprise that when we reunited, we spent hours walking around the Metropolitan Museum of Art doing what we had always done so easily thirty-five years ago: talk.

Our adorable Huck is still just as cute and lovable, and his new fame has not gone to his head. Huck is mostly a homebody and is happiest when eating, watching a ball game with Michael, or sleeping in his own little blue and red bed under the window. But he does always enjoy a walk along the East River near our house. Sometimes people recognize him as "the dog on the cover of that book!" but mostly he is stopped by passersby who are simply admiring his jaunty gait and his sweet face, always mistaking him for a puppy, even though he's now six years old.

After the publication of the book, some of the publicity events were more fun for Huck than others. He clearly has a preference for meeting families at libraries and bookstores and street fairs rather than going on TV. When we went on *The View,* Huck was so overwhelmed by the lights and the noise and the studio audience, he couldn't find a comfortable enough spot on my lap to sit still and relax. He spent most of the broadcast alternating between jumping out of my arms and frantically licking my face.

Huck showed up at Ramsey Day on a September

day in 2010 when the book was first published. It was Huck's first trip back to New Jersey since he slipped through the fence and started us all down a road we never would have imagined ourselves on. We all had a great time seeing the strangers who, for a seventy-two-hour period, had become our closest friends. People, especially children, were clamoring to get near Huck, to pet him and to hold him. Huck was very good-natured about it and did not at all seem to mind being passed from one set of arms to another all day long. Of course, Rich was always nearby, holding the leash tight, not taking any chances!

In truth, there is probably little chance that Huck would ever run away again. He hates to be without us, and reunions are always joyous affairs. Huck has an uncanny ability to anticipate just when those moments of separation are near, and it is always then that he chooses to be most playful.

For instance, every morning when Michael was still in high school, the moment he would move toward his backpack, Huck would bite into the straps and start pulling, putting his whole body—all nine pounds of himself—into trying to deter Michael from putting the pack on and heading off to school.

When I'm getting ready for work in the morning, Huck follows me around with a ball in his mouth. If I stop, Huck does, too, and drops the ball at my feet and stares up at me, just waiting for a game of fetch. Even after my coat is on and my hand is on the front door-knob, Huck, ball in mouth, continues his attempts to get me to stay home and play.

Michael is off to college now, having gotten through the late nights of homework during his high school years with Huck at his side, at his feet, and on his lap. Our apartment is a lot quieter, and Huck sometimes parks himself under the piano, seeming to be waiting for Michael to take his seat at the keyboard and fill our home with music again.

Huck has brought unparalleled joy into all our lives and is a constant reminder of the simple virtues that matter most in life—loyalty, humor, patience, compan-ionship, and unconditional love. He is also a reminder that joy may be just around the corner.

ACKNOWLEDGMENTS

I hope *Huck* will be a lasting testament to the kindness of the townspeople of Ramsey, Mahwah, Wyckoff, and Allendale who did not hesitate to extend a hand to strangers in need.

Huck is a part of the chapter of my life titled cancer. The unwavering support of *The New York Times* during my illness freed me to concentrate on getting well without anxiety that my role at the paper would be diminished. I am grateful to the paper's publisher, Arthur Sulzberger, and to my bosses Bill Keller, Jill Abramson, and John Geddes.

My deep gratitude to the doctors who have taken excellent care of me and made it easy for me to lower the journalist's raised eyebrow and trust them: Ann Carlon, Chip Cody, Catherine Hart, Tom Kolb, Beryl McCormick, and Anne Moore.

The affection, good humor, and thoughtful gestures—big and small—of many of my friends and colleagues lit the way through that very dark period in my life and its unsteady aftermath. My lifelong thanks to Rick Berke, Alison Bommarito, Sal Bommarito, Rachel Breitbart, Adam Bresnick, Orville Buddo, Dana Canedy, Dolly Cannon, Mary Ellen Caruso, Caroline Clarke, Marjorie Connelly, Brad Connor, Sharon Connor, Louise Conway, Peggy Conway, Maureen Dowd, Tonne Goodman, Alison Gwinn, Deborah Hofmann, Michael Kagay, Brian Kennedy, Dave Kepner, John Kepner, Mimi Kepner, Tim Kepner, Glenn Kramon, Mark Leibovich, Rich Meislin, Adam Nagourney, Patty Newburger, Todd Purdum, Joyce Purnick, Andy Rosenthal, Jane Rosenthal, Martin Rutishauser, Elaine Schattner, Susan Scott, Robert Sherman, Tammy Sherman, Ilde Smilen, Steve Smilen, Dick Stevenson, Dalia Sussman, David Sussman, Nina Tager, Megan Thee-Brenan, Angela Tortorella, Jeffrey Wilks, Lise Wilks, Donna Wilson, and Caren Zuckerman.

I pay tribute in these pages to dear friends whose hearts touched me and who died before their time: R. W. Apple, Connie Hays, David Kern, Bob Parisien, John Siskind, Ruth Sussman, and Robin Toner.

Much of *Huck* was written in the sun-lit rooms of the New York Society Library. My thanks to the staff there who provided me with a quiet place to think and work.

Three-quarters of the way through writing *Huck*, I fell off a horse and broke my elbow. My lasting gratitude to Emily Altman and Robert Hotchkiss for their world-class medical attention and to my friends Regina Lasko and David Letterman for their nonstop support. Together, they made it possible for me to finish the book in a timely way despite the cast that ran the length of my arm.

Though I loved *Huck*, I had no idea how it would be received. I put my fate in the hands of Christine Kay and Barbara Strauch, distinguished editors among distinguished editors at *The Times*, who good-naturedly took on the task of reading the manuscript in its earliest draft. I am indebted to them both.

It has been an honor to work with the talented people at Broadway Books. Christine Pride did a masterful job of gracefully editing *Huck* and, despite my protestations, was right to stand firm in her belief that readers want to know from the subtitle that the book they have just picked up has a happy ending. My thanks to Team *Huck* for their care, creativity, and infectious enthusiasm in launching *Huck* to a wide audience: Jacob Bronstein, Laura Duffy, Ellen Folan, Laurie McGee, Catherine Pollock, and Jennifer Robbins.

I am grateful to my literary agent, Esther Newberg, a prodder of authors but not a nagger, a vigilant e-mailer, who late one Sunday night found *Huck* among her electronic missives and decided it was a story that had to be told. She has been *Huck*'s champion and mine.

Larry Pinsky turned his camera on Huck and captured him in all his sweetness for the cover. I am grateful to him, to his wife, Elizabeth, and to Doris Kaplan for their concern and help during my illness.

Special thanks to Rick Finkelstein, Caroline Kennedy, Susan Scheftel, and Ed Schlossberg for their abiding friendship and for their daily ministrations to Rich, Michael, and me throughout the many difficult months of my cancer treatments.

Homage is due here to my parents and my siblings: to my father, William, whose love of books and dogs made its way down through the generations and into the heart of the grandson he did not live long enough to meet; and to my mother, Harriet, our loving Materfamilias, who has soldiered through a great deal of adversity with dignity and strength. Thanks to my brother, Bill, and my sister Louise for their unequivocal love, and for their support of *Huck* and all my endeavors. And thanks to Louise's husband, Joe, for standing with her.

As every *Huck* reader will attest, there could be no better pal to go through life with than my sister Barbara, from our childhood train rides on the stairs to our frantic search for Huck lost somewhere in the wild. My love and thanks to Barbara and her family: Dave, Justin, Kaitlyn, and Darian.

I know now what I should have known all those years ago, that a child's longing for a dog should not be taken lightly or dismissed as a matter of inconvenience. My son, Michael, has taught me more than I have taught him about what matters in life. His bravery, selflessness, and generous and joyful heart inspired me throughout our search for Huck and do so still.

Most of all, I am grateful to my adoring and adored husband, Rich. His intrepid spirit kept us moving forward, as it always does, despite the odds. There would be no story at all if not for his boundless love for his family and unshakable belief in the possible. Rich led us to Huck.